The Adoptee's Guide to Healing, Wholeness & Growth

LYNDA MONK, MSW, RSW, CPCC

Published by Books That Save Lives, an imprint of
Jim Dandy, Publishing, LLC

Cover Design: Ana Miller (anamillerdesign.com)

Interior Design: Jermaine Lau

Jim Dandy Publishing
6252 Peach Avenue
Van Nuys, CA 91411

info@jimdandypublishing.com

For bulk orders, special quantities, course adoptions, and
corporate sales, please email info@jimdandypublishing.com

ISBN (Print): 9781963667325, (ebook): 9781963667714

BISAC: FAM004000, SEL023000, FAM006000

"Adoption is an event that reverberates for a lifetime. In The Adoptee's Guide for Healing, Wholeness & Growth, Lynda Monk provides adoptees with a rich opportunity to reflect on their personal adoption story. As much workbook as journal, Monk's offering will touch every adoptee's heart—and serve them on their journey of reconciliation and self-acceptance. Highly recommended!"

—Eric Maisel, *Brave New Mind*

"Reading The Adoptee's Guide, I couldn't help but be drawn in. Lynda Monk's words and voice are honest, sincere, and compelling. Her self-awareness and personal anecdotes are so relatable, inviting deep empathy and connection. This book will touch many lives and support many adoptees' journeys to write and adapt their adoption story and discover self-love, acceptance and peace along the way."

—Ahava Shira, PhD,
memoir writer and wife of an adoptee.

"Honest and profoundly moving, Lynda Monk's, The Adoptee's Guide to Healing, Wholeness, & Growth lights the way toward understanding and self-acceptance. It's a compassionate and insightful roadmap for anyone seeking to understand the lifelong journey of adoption. It offers wisdom, honesty, and hope—inviting readers to embrace their story with courage and self-compassion. A must-read for anyone navigating the adoptee experience."

—Gregg Brown, MSc, PhD (in the making),
Speaker, Author, Adoptee

"As an adoptee, I found Lynda Monk's work deeply moving and supportive. Her willingness to share parts of her own journey brought comfort, validation, and insight to mine. This book offers thoughtful reflections and powerful questions that help normalize the complexities of adoption and open space for healing and self-understanding. As an occupational therapist who works with people navigating life's transitions, I recognize the profound impact of this work—it is compassionate, grounded, and transformative. This book is a gift for anyone who has been adopted - please read it."

—Anne Marie Hogya, Occupational Therapist, Movement Specialist, Adoptee

"Lynda Monk's The Adoptee's Guide to Healing, Wholeness & Growth is as incisive as it is filled with warmth and humility. It is as comprehensive about the stages in this journey as it is open and encouraging of surprises others will find as they journal. It is as honest about her adoptee journey as it is aware of the need for self-care when we write deeply. Reading this book, you will find you are in the hands of a skillfull coach and writer, an adoptee who has learned as she's journaled she is more than where she came from. As she shares from her pages, 'My life is a mosaic of family, moments, choices, and possibilities. I live and love it all. I want to remember the whole of who I am, always.'

The plentiful prompts in the book and the knowledge shared about finding one's self and being are valuable to any of us."

—Sheila Bender, *Since Then Poems and Short Prose* and *A New Theology: Turning to Poetry in a Time of Grief*

"Though not intended to be a therapeutic process, The Adoptee's Guide for Healing, Wholeness & Growth by Lynda Monk offers an opportunity to explore an often muted, and hushed topic. The questions raised in this workbook are valuable for both individuals and therapists searching for clarity and comprehension around adoption and the manifestation of its lifelong consequences."

—Chris Leischner M.S.W., R.S.W, B.A. Therapist

"Lynda Monk's *The Adoptee's Guide for Healing, Wholeness & Growth* is a masterwork of wisdom and guidance that reaches beyond even the diverse field of adoption. In this combination of psychological knowledge, personal story, and wonderful guided questioning and advising, Lynda unfolds the complexity of reckoning with personal history. In an organized progression, this book explores the themes of being an adoptee. These themes, including processing, healing, emotional complexity, attachment, empowerment, and self-compassion, are presented with extraordinary insight. Lynda's excerpts from her own journals light up the whole process. As she says, '...we swim in our own ocean defined by our own unique circumstances.' As the guide offers, these oceans can be treasure troves when approached with wholeness of heart, a pen, and a brilliant companion."

—Beth Jacobs, PhD, Psychologist and Author of *Writing For Emotional Balance*, *The Original Buddhist Psychology*, and *Luminous Loves Gray: poetry*.

"I loved reading this entire guide. I especially loved the last of Lynda's words 'I hope this adoptee healing guide and journal has helped you connect with your own story, or parts of it, in fresh, empowering and self-loving ways. I wish you much goodness on the part of your story that is not yet written or lived.' As soon as I finished, I knew I wanted to make a list of who I wanted to tell to read this book!"

—Joyce Chapman. author of *Journaling For Joy: Writing Your Way to Personal Growth and Freedom*

"Lynda Monk's *The Adoptee's Guide for Healing, Wholeness & Growth* is an insightful resource for adoptees on their path toward understanding, renewal, and self-discovery. The book provides a comprehensive approach with journaling tips and thoughtful prompts that facilitate reflection. Monk shares her own heartfelt journal entries to inspire adoptees to explore their personal experiences. Additionally, she emphasizes self-care practices to support readers as they work through their emotions.

By offering tools and encouragement, this guide creates opportunities for readers to explore their identity, honor their truths, and nurture personal growth. The Adoptee's Guide is more than just a workbook. It acts as a gentle companion, and through journaling, helps the reader discover the power of writing. I highly recommend this book for all adoptees, regardless of their experiences."

—Merle R. Saferstein, author of *Wisdom of the Century and Living* and *Leaving My Legacy, Vols. I and II.*

"The Adoptee's Guide is an extraordinary guide for adoptees, as well as for their families and friends, offering support and inspiration as they explore and grow through their unique stories. Written by Lynda Monk, a gifted leader in the coaching and journaling fields, this book weaves her experiences as an adoptee onto these pages with heartfelt wisdom and authenticity. Thoughtfully crafted prompts invite meaningful reflection, gently guiding readers toward healing, self-discovery, and positive growth. This guide and journal is truly a gift to us all!"

—Sandra Marinella, Writing teacher and author of *The Story You Need to Tell: Writing to Heal from Trauma, Illness, or Loss*

"In The Adoptee's Guide for Healing, Wholeness & Growth, Lynda Monk has written a beautiful and welcoming book. In clear, straight-forward language she invites readers to explore their own adoption journey. Written in a guided journal format, she shares a wide variety of concrete and specific exercises to help adoptees gently uncover their personal story. By sharing her own experience as an adoptee, she adds depth and understanding to the process of discovery."

—Susan Borkin, PhD, psychotherapist and author of *The Healing Power of Writing* and *When Your Heart Speaks, Take Good Notes*

"There are books that take years to write, and stories that wait patiently to be spoken. Within the pages of this intimate adoptee journal, Lynda has curated a body of work that speaks directly to the heart of the adoptee journey. I found myself reading slowly, pausing to absorb the depth of the quotes, many drawn from Lynda's own reflection and to take in the intimacy of the treasured pages from her personal journal. Her words read and tasted like medicine, offering balm to the tender places of the adoptee experience where questions of belonging, origin, and identity live.

This is an exquisitely crafted and deeply thoughtful work, one that offers healing and transformation for those ready to receive its abundance of wisdom and guidance. This is a journal that will change lives."

—Jackee Holder Coach, Author & Speaker & Co-Founder of The School Of Journaling (UK)

"Lynda Monk has written a heartwarming and inviting guide for adoptees to get in touch with a life milestone that is rarely referred to and is often kept secret: their adoption. The Adoptee's Guide offers a safe place to reflect with writing invitations, questions, and thought-provoking quotations. Lynda's journal excerpts offer insight from a fellow adoptee who knows 'our lives are defined both by what we have lost and what we carry.' She is an insightful and encouraging companion for the multi-layered experience of adoption and the journey of revealing one's innermost thoughts. How gratifying, and healing, it will be for adoptees to find out they're not alone."

—Mary Ann Moore, adoptive parent, writer, poet and writing mentor; author of *Writing to Map You Spiritual Journey*

"This insightful, informative guide gently leads adoptees on a journey of self-expression, discovery, and healing through reflective journaling. Author, journaling leader, and coach Lynda Monk poses thoughtful questions that invite pen to page, and graciously shares selections from her own journals, written in response to the book's evocative prompts. The Adoptee's Guide to Healing, Wholeness & Growth is a generous gift for those exploring their adoption journey."

—Judy Reeves, author of *When Your Heart Says Go*

"*The Adoptee's Guide for Healing, Wholeness & Growth* is an invaluable and warmhearted companion for anyone hoping to understand the many dimensions of their own experience as an adopted child. Lynda Monk's sensitive exploration of the challenges and emotional complexities of adoption are woven together with generous passages from her personal journals that offer fascinating glimpses of her lifelong adoptee's journey. Lynda emphasizes again and again that every adoptee's experience is unique and worthy of telling. If you are an adoptee, you will appreciate her loving encouragement and guidance to explore the richness of your own story as you read the book."

—Marlene Schiwy, Ph.D, author of *A Voice of Her Own* and *The Art of Creating Workshops for Women*

"Lynda Monk, who is one of the most authentic and gifted leaders I've ever worked with, has brought her signature clarity, compassion and style to a journaling guide for adoptees. Her gentle guidance through the often complex path of identity and belonging is sure to be a beacon of hope and resolve. With dozens of insightful journal prompts and candid excerpts from her own adoptee journal, she shines with the light of one who has come to know herself with certainty and now passes on the gift."

—Kathleen Adams LPC, Founder, Center for Journal Therapy and author, *Journal to the Self*.

Books by the Author

Affirmations for Self-Love: A Motivational Journal with Prompts for Self-Worth, Self-Acceptance & Positive Self-Talk (2024) co-authored with Eric Maisel, PhD

The Coach's Guide to Completing Creative Work: Top Tips for Working with Procrastination, Perfectionism and More (2023) co-edited with Eric Maisel, PhD

The Great Book of Journaling: How Journal Writing Can Support a Life of Wellness, Creativity, Meaning and Purpose (2022) co-edited with Eric Maisel, PhD

Transformational Journaling for Coaches, Therapists, and Clients: A Complete Guide to the Benefits of Personal Writing (2021) co-edited with Eric Maisel, PhD

Writing Alone Together: Journalling in a Circle of Women for Creativity, Compassion and Connection (2014) co-authored with Wendy Judith Cutler, MA and Ahava Shira, PhD

Dedication

For adoptees everywhere,

you belong here.

And to all those who love us wholeheartedly.

Disclaimer

The Adoptee's Guide to Healing, Wholeness & Growth offers many journaling prompts for exploration. Journaling is not therapy, but it can be very therapeutic and healing. It is important to allow yourself to be resourced and supported while you do this type of suggested reflective journaling. You might even consider letting someone you trust know that you are writing in this guided journal so you can ask for support when it gets difficult or you are expressing deep emotions.

If ever you need to process some of what you are reflecting and journaling about, or find any parts of it distressing, please seek counselling or support of some kind for your healing journey and your well-being as an adoptee. This guide does not serve as counselling or mental health support. Please note there are some self-care tips provided to support you with your healing, growth, and journaling journey.

ACKNOWLEDGMENTS

My thanks to the following people who have supported me and the creation of *The Adoptee's Guide to Healing, Wholeness & Growth*, including...

Peter Allan, my husband, personal editor, and greatest supporter. Our two sons, Jackson and Jesse Allan, who make me want to do and be my best every single day. I am truly grateful to be their mother.

Eric Maisel, my colleague and friend, who first said, "You should send your idea for this journal to Brenda." We have published four books together and I look forward to another one, whatever it shall be. He is the author of more than sixty books, so I am confident there will indeed be a next one!

Brenda Knight, thank you for saying yes when I sent the idea for this project your way, and for your support as I brought it into being. When you said it will be "one for the ages," you made my heart sing.

Thanks also to all members of the Books That Save Lives team.

Sincere thanks to Kate Campbell, a fellow adoptee and talented greeting card artist, for inspiring the cover of this book. To Ana Miller, thanks for creating the final cover design. You both are part of the art and heart that wraps this book with beauty and intention.

Gratitude to Kimberly Wulfert for her feedback on the cover, it helped take it to the finish line.

Thanks to fellow adoptees Julie Ryan McGue for the wonderful foreword. and Juliana J Bruno for the afterword.

Thank you to my trusted friends, who are also fellow adoptees, who served as first readers and advisors, including Anne Marie Hogya, Gregg Brown, and Wendy Roberts. Gratitude to Jane Timleck, another reviewer and one of my first colleagues when I worked in child welfare in my early social work career. She went on to work with the Children's

Aid Society in Ontario for thirty-one years, twenty of those years in adoption, and she was a permanency planning specialist for part of that time. Thanks also to my dear friends and reviewers Chris Leischner, Linda Dobson, and Ahava Shira for their support and valuable input. Thanks to Kelly-Ann Spezowka, and the "Greek Goddesses," for brainstorming titles together while overlooking the sea.

Thanks to everyone within our International Association for Journal Writing (IAJW.org) community, including many of the Journal Council members who offered endorsements for this guide. Connection fuels our creativity. I'm inspired by the transformational power of going to the page, individually and together.

My gratitude to Lorraine Gane, whose encouragement of me as a writer has been a meaningful presence in my life for many years.

While they can no longer receive my gratitude directly, as my dad is no longer in this world and my mom suffers from advanced Alzheimer's disease, my deepest thanks go to my loving parents, Doug and Marion Monk, who made me their daughter through adoption. Love to my brother Jeff Monk, also an adoptee, and to our extended family members who have loved us as their own all our lives.

I am grateful to my biological mother, Diane Antkiw, who brought me into this world. Thanks to the Rosehart family, who have shown me love. Thanks to Diane for reading the draft of this book and for saying she liked it. Her story is also part of my story, and I'm grateful to have her blessing to share it.

Lastly, I want to acknowledge my biological father, Rob Fletcher. Sadly, he was no longer in this world when I learned his identity. But I have been enriched to recently find the Fletcher family, including my two "new brothers" Chad and Ryan Fletcher, and someday I also hope to meet my biological half-sister, Kirstin. Adoption reunions, and all the layers and years and people that they weave together, can take time...an entire lifetime!

Table of Contents

ROOTS

Coming into awareness of your adoption

RECOGNITION

Acknowledging emotional impacts and

RESILIENCE

RELATIONSHIPS

RECLAIM

REMEMBER

RADIANCE

FOREWORD

JULIE RYAN MCGUE

Adoptee and author of *Twice a Daughter, Twice the Family,* and *Belonging Matters.*

If you're holding this book, chances are adoption has shaped your life in ways you're still trying to understand. As an adoptee, I know how quietly—and persistently—those questions can live inside us. They surface at unexpected moments, linger without clear answers, and shift as we grow and change over time.

I am a writer, a lifetime journaler, and an adoptee. I was adopted as an infant, along with my twin sister, into a loving family. From the outside, our story looked complete. And in many ways, it was. But as I grew older, questions remained—about identity, origins, and what it means to belong to more than one family narrative at the same time.

For decades, I didn't consider looking into my adoption story. It wasn't until a health issue forced me to confront the limits of my medical history that I began searching for my birth relatives. That decision opened a door I could not close again. What followed was not a straight path or a single emotional experience, but a series of moments marked by hope, uncertainty, rejection, and eventually, connection. My birth relative's initial hesitation and distance were painful. Their later willingness to know me, and to reunite, required courage on all sides.

Incorporating those experiences—being adopted, searching, being rejected, and then welcomed—into any psyche is a complex feat, however well-adjusted one may be. I have long admired the social workers and professionals who walk alongside birth relatives and adoptees during these fragile moments, helping piece together what was once lost or hidden. There is nothing simple about adoption search, reunion or reconnection. There is no single roadmap that fits everyone.

What helped me most during those years was writing. Journaling gave me a place to sit with complexity—to tell the truth without rushing it, to explore feelings that did not cancel each other out, and to make sense of experiences that unfolded slowly and unevenly. Writing did not fix anything, but it helped me stay present and grounded as my story continued to unfold.

It was during this period of reflection and writing that I first met Lynda Monk in her role with IAJW. She invited me to speak to one of her groups after my adoption search memoir, *Twice a Daughter: A Search for Identity, Family, and Belonging*, was released in 2021. From the outset, I respected her thoughtful approach and her deep understanding of how journaling supports healing. As a social worker and fellow adoptee, Lynda recognizes that adoptee stories live in layers and that reflection takes time. I have followed her work ever since because I trust the care and integrity she brings to this field.

That care is evident throughout *The Adoptee's Guide to Healing, Wholeness and Growth*.

This book does not simplify adoption or promise easy answers. Instead, it offers a steady framework for reflection through themes such as Roots, Recognition, Resilience, Relationships, Reclaiming, Remembering, and Radiance. These are not steps to complete, but places to pause—touchstones readers can return to as life changes and new understandings emerge.

What I appreciate most about this guide is its respect for the adoptee experience. Healing is not framed as fixing something broken, but as tending to what has been carried—sometimes quietly—for years. Reflective journaling becomes a way to work through moments of loss, connection, confusion, and growth with honesty and care.

I am grateful that Lynda Monk created this guide, and I am glad you are here with it. Choosing to engage with *The Adoptee's Guide to Healing, Wholeness and Growth* is a meaningful gift to yourself—a decision to give your story the time and compassion it deserves. May this journal support you as you reflect, heal, and grow, and remind you that this work unfolds with patience, care, and time.

INTRODUCTION

Every adoptee's experience is unique. My hope is that you
will find some common threads of relatability, validation, and
understanding within the pages of this guide and journal. I
have created it with intention and care especially for fellow
adoptees who want to know, grow, and care for themselves.

Before this journey begins, I want to say a few things
about adoption itself, to offer a wide-lens view, so that you
might see yourself here, in your own unique experience as
an adoptee.

About Adoption

We each have our own unique adoption stories and
experiences that exist within the larger landscape of adoption.
In its essence, adoption is a legal and emotional process
by which a person or persons assume permanent parental
responsibility for a child who is not biologically their own.
But adoption is far more than simply a legal arrangement; it's
a deeply personal, lifelong journey that can affect identity,
relationships, and emotional well-being. By its very nature,
adoption involves gaining one family at the cost of another.

There are so many different types of adoption experiences,
including but not limited to the following:

- Open adoption
- Closed adoption
- Kin adoption
- 2SLGBTQI+ adoption
- Trans-racial adoption
- Intercultural adoption
- International adoption
- Foster-to-adopt
- Secret adoptions
- Adoption into families that have both biological and
  adopted children

- Adoptions that went well, which are often called "successful adoptions"
- Adoptions that did not go well, which are often called "unsuccessful adoptions"
- Adoption breakdowns
- Adoption reunions

The result is the commonly-referred-to "adoption triangle," which includes all parties involved: the biological parents, the adoptive parents, and the adoptee.

This guide is devoted to those of us who are adoptees, honoring that we each have our own unique adoption stories and experiences; we each have our own unique adoption triangles. All adoption triangles ultimately have their own look and feel.

While adoption has universal elements, its diversity is equally important to acknowledge and respect. I have met so many fellow adoptees in my life and work. I have met people who were placed for adoption at birth, were adopted by loving adoptive parents, and have had reunions with biological parents. I have known others who were not so much given up for adoption as taken and raised as a child to grandparents or aunts, as if those people were their biological parents, and the adoptee was never told the truth, but learned it some other way. I have known adoptees who were literally abandoned as babies and left at the front doors of fire stations or other places, presumably by a birth mom who was not able to keep her child, leaving her infant somewhere in the hopes they could have a better life. I have known adoptees who never learned they were adopted until they were adults, which can add a whole layer of betrayal and confusion to their lives.

Adoptions can happen after tragic losses of parents, or because of various circumstances at different ages in a child's life. For example, many years ago, I was a temporary foster parent to a young boy whose father was in prison and whose mother suffered from addiction and was unhoused, living on the streets, while a foster-to-adopt home was being sought for him and his sister. There are foster-to-adopt placements that work out and ones that don't.

While this journal is not a deep dive into adoption, I want us to understand that there is an ocean-sized world that adoption lives in. As adoptees, we swim in our own ocean, defined by our own unique circumstances.

While there is no one path as an adoptee, neither from where we start or where we go, the same is true for most people—we all have origin stories, family stories, and the stories of our childhood-to-adulthood journeys. One thing we share as adoptees is often the question of identity—where do we come from? Who are we, really? What roles do nature and nurture play in who we are?

Maybe you always loved to paint or make art, but neither of your parents are artists, and you always wondered where you got that part of yourself. Subsequently, you learn your biological parents were artists, or very creative, and it is like a missing piece of who you are arrives, bit by bit, as you learn about your biological roots.

Just as there is no one adoption experience, there are also numerous circumstances, and desires, around learning more about our biological roots as adoptees. For example, there might be a quiet or out loud search for our roots and where we come from, for some of us, as adoptees. Other adoptees may have no interest whatsoever in learning about their biological roots and would never want to have an adoption reunion. There are open adoptions, where some of that history has always been available to an adoptee, and where first families and second families all know one another right from the beginning of the adoption journey.

As adoptees, we are all unique! We walk our own path, and have our own family circumstances, just as any person does. But, perhaps, we have an extra notch in our life belt, a notch that we either tighten, fill, or bypass in some way as adoptees.

Once an adoptee, always an adoptee; we are never not that. How much this part of our reality and identity matters or factors into our choices, our happiness, how we live our life, what we search for, how we love ourselves and others, how we feel about our family tree and generations past and present, how we feel about identity and belonging, can all filter through the "adoptee lens" and our experiences as adoptees.

My Adoption Story, Briefly...

I was born in Kitchener, Ontario, Canada, on September 11, 1969. In those days, adoption records were sealed and closed. Over the years, the adoption laws evolved, and once it became possible for closed adoption records to be opened, I applied to get my "non-identifying adoption information" from those opened records when I was twenty.

I learned that I had been born to an eighteen-year-old girl who could not keep me as her own. I learned that I was in a foster home for the first five months of my life, until I was adopted by my parents. They were delayed in bringing me home as I was sick at the time. I always wondered why they couldn't get me when I was sick, as if they wouldn't be able to care for a sick child.

My parents told me and my brother—also an adoptee, from a different family of origin—that we were both adopted when we were young children. I was about six and Jeff, my brother, was around four, at the time. I still remember us sitting on either side of our dad, on the edge of my bed, when he explained that we were both adopted. He said that we had been born to our moms, and that they weren't able to keep us, and that they were able to become our mom and dad instead. My mom was standing nearby while we were given this explanation. My dad finished off this story by saying that we shouldn't tell anyone about this. My brother and I both nodded and said, "Okay." Our being adopted was not discussed much after that—until I was in second grade and accidentally told my whole class I was adopted, but that is another story.

About This Guide

I remember, in my early years as a social worker, reading somewhere that *to heal means to make whole*. There is no single way to strive for our sense of healing and wholeness as adoptees, but rather there are many psychological and emotional touchstones that might be part of our healing journeys.

This Adoptee's Guide strives to help you reflect on some of these touchstones through your own self-reflection and expressive writing.

Expressive writing heals. It includes writing about our thoughts and feelings as honestly and openly as we can. It is about the process not perfection, and it is personal to you. Journaling is getting what is on the inside out, so you have new perspective, release emotions, and gain new self-understanding and personal growth.

This is intended to be a guide, filled with journaling prompts that are invitations, questions, and inquiries to gently take you into yourself and your adoptee story for healing, wholeness, and growth. In addition to the journaling prompts, it offers inspiring and thought-provoking quotes, short reflections on the key topics, and excerpts from the pages of my journal as examples of going to the page. These excerpts are sprinkled throughout this journal to share some of my adoptee story with you, in the hopes they offer encouragement and companionship as you connect with your own adoptee story.

A Word About Words

I often say there is a whole world in a single word. There are three intentionally chosen words in the title of this journal that I want to shine a light on before we move forward, and these include healing, wholeness, and growth. These are all subjective ideas, and can mean different things to each one of us, as adoptees and as individuals. While this is true, it is also true that there are some key elements that can help us achieve healing, wholeness, and growth. This guide and journal strives to share some of these elements through the many topics and touchstones offered.

I want to say more about healing before we move forward. Firstly, some people might not even like the word *healing*, as it might conjure the idea that something is broken and needs to be fixed. Or they might not even relate to having an "adoption wound" to begin with, and hence healing is not needed, or it feels irrelevant to them.

Healing, to me, is part of our human experience. We all face different challenges and pains in our lives that can be emotional, physical, psychological, spiritual, and existential in nature. I believe healing is how we come back to center, how we honor our wholeness, how we tend to our overall feelings of well-being, and how we evolve into the fullness of who we are here to be in this lifetime. I think healing includes all the actions we take to feel okay with who we are and who we are becoming. And that, even if we are not feeling or doing okay, at times, our healing practices remind us that we can cope, we can manage, we can survive, we can still live well, or well enough, even in challenging times.

We have all likely heard the expression that time heals all wounds. I'm not sure I totally agree with that. I think time can distance us from the acuteness of our wounds; for example, grief can potentially lessen over time, or get a little more in the rear-view mirror of our lives. But it just takes that one song to play, that one memory to resurface, and grief can feel immediate and real in the moment. And so, healing and holding on and letting go and coping continues.

I think it takes more than time to heal adoptee wounds, or any psychological or emotional wound, for that matter. It is not like a broken bone that gets set, cast, and in a few weeks has fused together again, and the healing is complete. Emotional wounds can be triggered and reactivate in our mind, body, heart, and spirit at any time through the years.

I have grown to believe that true healing involves reflection, insight-building, and releasing. Healing happens when we deepen our understanding of our experiences and can reframe them, re-story them in empowering ways. Healing doesn't happen without some sort of processing, choosing, and releasing, without validation, compassion, and care. Things can fester in us, but they can also be cleared and released.

This is where journaling comes in! Journaling is a powerful reflective practice that helps build self-awareness and insight, especially when it is intentionally used for these very purposes, as it is presented here in this adoptee guide.

How to Use This Guide

There are many ways to journal, including free writing. Free writing involves writing whatever comes into your mind and heart at any given time, without censoring it or judging what you write. You simply write and trust where the writing takes you. This is often what we understand journaling to be, a place for unstructured self-expression where whatever you write is right!

In this guide, I am offering you some structure and guidance for your journaling and expressive writing. The prompts are intentional for your self-reflection, to support your emotional exploration and deepen your self-understanding. These prompts are aligned with, and informed by, some of the key emotional and psychological areas that adoptees often navigate throughout their lives in different ways.

The journaling prompts are presented within broader themes that, while not universal, are common enough to touch on many aspects of healing and growth for adoptees. You will know best which themes and areas of reflection matter most. Be patient and kind with yourself, and with the journaling process itself.

Healing the "adoption wound," sometimes referred to as the "abandonment wound" or the "primal wound," often involves reclaiming one's story, building safe connections and containers for growth. This guide is intended as a safe container for your self-reflection. Learn to hold both the pain and the strength that comes from being adopted. Remember, you are journaling to heal and grow, and your journaling is a safe space where your inner child, your present self, and your wise self can meet and be heard. You can write about your past experiences, your present circumstances, and your hopes for the future as you journal. You can write across all time and space. Let your journal be your witness, your friend, and your companion.

Healing and growth are not one-and-done experiences; they are lifelong choices to live whole, healthy, and self-aware lives. This journal can help you meet yourself where you are, at any stage of life, at any milestone of growth along the way. You can even return to this journal in years to come, to reflect from the perspective that only your future self can offer.

Allow this to be a gentle process, with self-compassion, self-care, and willingness to grow leading the way page by page. Let this journaling process ripple goodness and growth out into your whole self and your whole life, word by word.

Get a Companion Journal

While there is space provided for you to journal with the prompts provided in this book, there is only a small space offered to explore potentially big questions and musings. I encourage you to get another journal that you can expand into as you work your way through the themes and prompts offered. This separate journal can be devoted to your adoptee journaling journey, and you can turn there to write from the prompts that you want more space to explore.

About the Journaling Prompts

There is a transformational power in good and intentional questions. The journal prompts offered here are powerful questions, to open you to your reflections, curiosities, insights, and aha moments. They are intended to support you in understanding and integrating your unique experiences as an adoptee. This can offer you healing, inspiration, and nourishment for your whole self in mind, body, heart, and spirit.

Practice Self-Care When Journaling

When journaling about potentially emotional topics as an adoptee, where you might feel triggered or uncomfortable, it's essential to practice compassionate self-care. Writing can bring deep healing, but it can also surface pain, grief, anger, or confusion. Allowing yourself to identify and express your emotions freely can help bring about healing, resilience, and growth.

Be with what is, without any judgment, as you write and express yourself. Write, breathe, and write some more. Writing begins with the breath. It is tender ground to write about our experiences as adoptees. It is also healing and empowering to go on such a journey for *and* with yourself.

Five self-care strategies for your journaling journey:

1. **Create a safe and supportive space to journal**

   - Choose a quiet, private space, where you feel emotionally and physically safe and comfortable, to write. You may consider having soft lighting, calming music, a cozy blanket, and a warm cup of tea. I love journaling with my dog, Sadie, curled beside me on the couch. Choose what makes you feel comfortable and supported, and try to include those things in your journaling environment.

2. **Acknowledge that all your feelings are valid**

   - It is important to give yourself permission to feel what you feel. There is no "wrong" emotion. Emotions like grief, anger, confusion, sadness, as well as love, joy, and gratitude, can all be part of our experience as adoptees. You may never have expressed your true emotions as an adoptee. This is your chance to connect with how you feel, and honor your feelings without judgment and with self-compassion and care.

3. **Set boundaries around your journaling**

   - You might like to decide ahead of time how long you'll write in this journal at any one time (e.g., fifteen to thirty minutes). There is no need to pressure yourself to push through, or to expect yourself to go deep every time you write. Also, if the writing feels difficult or emotionally triggering, it's okay to stop and return to it another time. You can pace yourself. You are in control of your own journaling process, and it is essential to listen to your inner cues and wisdom around this.

   - Our own journaling can take us by surprise, sometimes, with the places it can take us! That is part of the joy of journaling, all the wonderful rich and wandering places we can go on the page and within ourselves. That can also be difficult sometimes. There have been times when I was journaling and it seemed easy, and all of a sudden, out of the blue, my writing took me to a place that felt more vulnerable. It took me to a place I didn't want to go in that moment.

   - If your journaling ever feels overwhelming, you can choose to stick with it, or pause, or stop altogether! You can always come back to it later—healing and growth doesn't happen all once.

   - As my friend and journaling colleague Kay Adams teaches, it is important to consider pacing, structure, and containment with our journaling. Timed writing can give us some of that structure; prompts can also give us structure and containment. Pace yourself!

4. **Balance reflection with self-nurturing**

   - While journaling can be a very self-nurturing and self-caring practice, it can also be heavy sometimes, especially if we are writing about emotionally charged or deeply personal or challenging topics. In this journal, when you are reflecting on your formative experiences as an adoptee, you aren't writing about the weather or what you did today; you are writing with gentle prompts calling you forth to write to heal, know, and grow yourself. This type of intentional self-expressive practice needs to be done with a balanced approach.

- For example, if you have been writing about something emotionally stirring or difficult, you can balance that with writing about something uplifting, grounding, or soothing. Write about a memory or moment that made you feel loved, cherished, or connected. Write about something you are grateful for in the moment. You might even write small affirmations along the way, for example, "My feelings are valid and worthy of expression."
- I have often found, when journaling about my experience as an adoptee, that many truths, even paradoxes, emerge at once.

FROM THE PAGES OF MY JOURNAL

I am so happy and grateful that I found and met Diane (my birth mother). I'm always so grateful when we are together. I also feel sad when we have to say good-bye. Sadder than when I say good-bye to most other people. Perhaps our separation will always have a trigger of loss to it. Sometimes our togetherness has that same sadness too, not for the being together, but for the reminder of all the years we spent apart. Grief and gratitude always feel present whether we are together or apart. I believe she feels this too.

5. Ground yourself before and after writing

- I created a transformational journaling method called Life Source Writing, which has five steps, including arrive, relax, write, reflect, and affirm. It suggests a couple of steps before we begin to write, including *arriving fully* and *relaxing*. Arriving is a moment of mindfulness, where you simply acknowledge that you are showing up for yourself and your time to journal. You can affirm with quiet inner statements, such as, "*I am here now to take time for myself to write and reflect.*"

- This can help you settle into the moment and be fully present. Next is intentionally relaxing and engaging the relaxation response in your mind and body. You can do something simple, like taking a few deep breaths, allowing your exhale to be longer than your inhale. You can place your hand over your heart and imagine breathing in comfort, care, and calm. You can ground yourself by noticing the surface beneath you, the chair or couch or whatever you are sitting on, and imagining that surface supporting you and holding you as you write.

- Likewise, do simple things to soothe and ground after you write. Think of easy things that feel calming to you—perhaps taking a short walk, or sitting out in nature, or hugging a pet or loved one, or calling a trusted friend. I often take a couple of minutes after I journal to quietly meditate and come home to myself and the moment, after being engaged on the page.

- You will find what works for you, but the invitation here is to center, ground, and nourish yourself before and after you journal. These calming and mindful practices can enrich your journaling and support your well-being.

Create Your Own Journaling Self-Care Plan

Pause, Reflect & Journal

Let these writing prompts support you...

- How do you want to care for yourself on your adoptee journaling journey?

- What helps you feel grounded if you feel overwhelmed by adoption-related emotions?
- What brings you feelings of peace and calm?
- What can help you feel safe and supported for your inner reflection and journaling time?
- What else would you like to keep in mind, and do, for your self-care?

Enter an Oasis in Your Journal

"The blank page is like an oasis, a space that can hold you safe and still while you take time to write, reflect, and grow."

—LYNDA MONK

I invite you to give yourself permission to let journaling be like entering your own oasis. Let it be easy and enjoyable. Know you can support yourself and make choices if it ever feels difficult. Trust that your self-expression is meaningful, and that it can bring deep peace and greater joy into your life in very real and sustaining ways. Imagine your journaling practice as your constant companion, as an adoptee and as a whole person, where being an adoptee is just part of who you are, just part of your experience. You are that, and so much more!

FROM THE PAGES OF MY JOURNAL

I carry my adoptee experience with me, but it does not carry all of me. I am more than where I came from and I am that too. My life is a mosaic of family, moments, choices, and possibilities. I live and love it all. I want to remember the whole of who I am, always.

"Your heart is the size of an ocean. Go find yourself in its hidden depths."

—RUMI

THE ADOPTEE JOURNALING JOURNEY

Introducing the Reflective Journaling Themes

In this guide, I will invite you to explore various themes that can support your healing, wholeness, and growth journey as an adoptee. The themes and journaling prompts are offered in categories, which can also be thought of as phases we might go through on our healing, growth, and self-discovery paths as adoptees. That path begins with your roots and coming into awareness of your adoption experience; it recognizes core wounds, then moves to resilience and relationships, and eventually through to reclaim and remember, where you deepen understanding, move to integration, and touch into your radiance, and empowerment and peace, which can come at any moment of acceptance through this process.

Your journaling journey will explore these healing pathways:

- ROOTS *coming into awareness of your adoption experience*
- RECOGNITION *acknowledging emotional impacts and processing*
- RESILIENCE *connecting with inner strength*
- RELATIONSHIPS *building meaningful connections and understanding attachment*
- RECLAIM *belonging, integration, and empowerment*
- REMEMBER *honoring growth and wholeness*
- RADIANCE *living with love and making peace*

The flow through these themes or phases isn't rigid. Healing is spiral shaped, not linear. There might be some of these areas of exploration that don't resonate with you, that's fine, just skip them. Be with these explorations and reflections in a way that works for you. Choose as you go along where you want to stop, pause, dip in, dive deeper, or simply turn the page and go on by. This is your journal. Your journey. Your life. Your unique experience as an adoptee. Let's touch our toes to the water now and begin!

ROOTS
Coming into awareness of your adoption experience

In the ROOTS section of this guide, you are invited to explore:

- Your Adoption Story
- Being
- Awareness
- Awakening
- Identity
- Truth
- Rooted

YOUR ADOPTION STORY

*"An adoption story isn't just a chapter,
it's a lifelong unfolding of identity, love, and truth."*

—LYNDA MONK

We all have our own unique adoption and adoptee stories. We live our stories. Our stories are our life. We have the parts of the story we have authored ourselves, and we have the stories that have been given to us. Quite often, in adoptee stories, there are a lot of missing pieces, and sometimes plots that might feel like they don't quite add up. Sometimes they are simple stories, sometimes very complicated, and ultimately, each of them is complex in its own way. This is inherently true because the story has a plot line that includes being separated from our original, or birth, parents and families of origin. That in itself is, well, complicated. Not bad or good, just complicated. Take time to reflect on your own adoption story with the help of the following journaling prompts

JOURNALING PROMPTS

What is my adoption story?

What are some of the particulars of this story? When was I adopted? Who was I adopted by?

_____

_____

_____

_____

_____

_____

_____

_____

_____

What do I know about my origin story?

_____

_____

_____

_____

_____

_____

_____

_____

_____

_____

When did I learn I was adopted? Who told me?

_____

_____

_____

_____

_____

_____

_____

What questions about my adoption story remain
unanswered, if any? How do I live with those questions?

_____

_____

_____

_____

_____

_____

_____

_____

_____

_____

How much of my story do I feel I truly know, and how much feels like a mystery?

_____

_____

_____

_____

_____

_____

_____

_____

What stories have I told myself about my adoption, and are they still true for me now?

_____

_____

_____

_____

_____

_____

_____

_____

What is it like to think about my own adoption story?
How do I feel? What do I notice?

BEING

"You were someone before you were adopted. You are someone still. Your being has always mattered."

—LYNDA MONK

Being is one of the most profound and foundational concepts in our human experience. It refers to our very state of existence, of simply being alive, and it includes our awareness of our own aliveness. It includes our presence, being in the moment, being fully here, and being fully ourselves. We all want to be seen, to be known, and to be valued for simply existing. So often we focus on what we are doing, or what we need to do, but being is a more still state, an essence state. Being does not require any specific action; it is deeper than that, it is fundamentally the very essence of you.

JOURNALING PROMPTS

How central is being an adoptee to my self-understanding and my identity?

When have I felt proud, confused, angry, or sad about being adopted? What triggered those feelings?

How would I describe myself beyond the label of "adoptee?"

How does being present look and feel to me?

_____

_____

_____

_____

_____

_____

_____

_____

FROM THE PAGES OF MY JOURNAL

The essence of the concept of "being" can be a hard concept to grasp. It makes me think of the difference between a human "doing" and a human "being." For a long time, I felt my sense of worth was related to how much I was doing, or accomplishing, or contributing, as these things were very valued in my family. I once heard a coaching client, who was a busy and burned-out leader and a fellow adoptee, say, "I truly believe my identity and worth are in direct relationship to how much I do, just being is not enough." In that moment, I remember asking her, "What if it was enough?"

AWARENESS

*"Self-awareness is the foundation of emotional
intelligence and a cornerstone of growth."*

—DANIEL GOLEMAN

Coming into deeper awareness about our adoptee experience
is about truth, compassion, and ownership of our story.
This awareness about our adoption experiences can awaken
healing and growth, and this naturally layers throughout
our lives. Awareness is not about fixing; it is about noticing.
From that observation of our experiences as they were and
are, growth can happen. We are not just gaining awareness
about our experience as adoptees; we are gaining overall
self-awareness!

JOURNALING PROMPTS

What messages did I receive growing up, directly
or indirectly, about my adoption, and how did
those shape me?

How does awareness help me connect my past, present, and future?

What am I becoming aware of in myself that I couldn't see or feel before?

_____

_____

_____

_____

_____

_____

_____

_____

_____

How is this awareness shifting the way I relate to myself and my adoption story?

_____

_____

_____

_____

_____

_____

_____

_____

FROM THE PAGES OF MY JOURNAL

For years, I didn't think much about being adopted. I just thought it meant that we were chosen (as that is what we were told), and that made us special. But I realized, as years went on and I got older, it also meant seeing parts of my experience that I was never encouraged to talk about or feel anything about. This awareness didn't make me love my family any less or feel angry with them, it just made me a bit more curious about what was missing and who I was and how I truly felt as an adoptee. I began to ask more questions about where I came from. At the time, there were no real answers to these questions. The questions themselves started me on a path to find answers.

AWAKENING

"Awakening is not changing who you are, but discarding who you are not."

—DEEPAK CHOPRA

Awakening as an adoptee often begins with a quiet inner stirring. Maybe you have this subtle sense that there's more to the story of who you are than what's been told or acknowledged, more than anyone knows or can tell you. It may start with a question, a feeling, or a moment of life transition that brings deeper emotions to the surface. Awakening is not necessarily a single moment, but perhaps more of a feeling, and when it happens, we might embrace some parts of ourselves and shed others. Perhaps the real journey of awakening is not so much about embracing or shedding or discarding; rather, awakening can involve expansion, by opening to more truths, to more of who we truly are.

JOURNALING PROMPTS

What does awakening mean to me as an adoptee?

_____

_____

_____

_____

_____

_____

_____

What questions have I had as an adoptee? What answers have I looked for?

What specific moment of awakening as an adoptee do I recall, if any?

_____

_____

_____

_____

_____

_____

_____

_____

_____

_____

What is one truth I want to carry forward as I continue this awakening journey?

_____

_____

_____

_____

_____

_____

FROM THE PAGES OF MY JOURNAL

I've often had the feeling of awakening as an adoptee. These moments where I felt like I was learning more about who I am and where I come from. With these awakening moments, it's been like this process of unfolding myself and finding new parts in the folds themselves.

This happened with literal folds in the sheets of a bed. The first time I spent the night with my birth mom, we were in a hotel room together in Las Vegas—a trip we took to "get to know each other." We got into our respective hotel beds and, at the exact same moment, we sat up to pull the tightly tucked sheets out from the bottom of the bed, because neither one of us liked that feeling and preferred the sheets to be loose. We both instantly looked at each other, and started to laugh, recognizing ourselves in each other. It was such a rare sensation, to be like the other, so instinctively.

This moment awakened something deep within me that has lasted for over twenty years. A feeling of undeniable connection. I lay awake in the dark for a long time that night, wondering what it might be like to have that feeling as a child in one's own biological family. To be like your parents in some innate way. I also wondered what Diane was thinking, what it was like for her to fall asleep with her daughter in the next bed beside her, with sheets loose at her feet just like her.

IDENTITY

"Identity can be many things."

—AHAVA SHIRA

It is an innate human experience to ask, "Who am I?" Our identity shapes our understanding of who we are and how we see ourselves. It is shaped by many factors, including our values, beliefs, personality, experiences, roles, and connections. It involves our culture, ethnicity, gender, sexuality, family, upbringing, relationships, choices, interests, and passions. Having a sense of identity is deeply important, as it influences our mental, emotional, physical, and relational well-being. It gives us that sense of inner stability and continuity across time in our lives, including the past, present, and future. When or if we lack a sense of identity due to life circumstances, including adoption, we might experience anxiety, depression, insecurity, struggles with confidence, difficulty trusting others, and feeling like we don't belong. Identity is never static; rather, it's an evolving understanding of yourself over time.

Identity can be discovered, reclaimed, and nurtured as adoptees. It's deeply healing to say, "This is who I am, and I get to define that."

It can start by looking in the mirror and truly seeing ourselves for who we are.

Being adopted can shape how we see ourselves, our worth, and our place in the world in ways that others might not always understand—even in ways that we ourselves might not always fully understand.

JOURNALING PROMPTS

In what ways has being adopted shaped the way I
see myself?

What parts of my identity feel clear to me and what
parts feel uncertain?

What were some of the first messages I received about who I was supposed to be?

_____

_____

_____

_____

_____

_____

_____

_____

When I look in the mirror I see...

_____

_____

_____

_____

_____

_____

_____

_____

_____

_____
_____
_____
_____
_____
_____
_____
_____
_____
_____

FROM THE PAGES OF MY JOURNAL

My mom has forgotten, not just us, but also herself, as she lives with late-stage Alzheimer's disease. She no longer knows who she is when she sees her reflection in the mirror, sometimes asking "Who's that?" when she catches a glimpse of herself.

I wonder what it must be like for her to look in the mirror and not know who she is.

I had that feeling before, actually. I would look in the mirror as a young girl and stare at my reflection and wonder where my blue eyes came from, or my height, or the shape of my smile, the colour of my skin...Who made me?

These aren't small things to wonder about. Where do I come from? What am I made of? Who am I? What is the truth of who I see in the mirror?

TRUTH

"The truth is rarely pure and never simple."

—OSCAR WILDE

There is healing that can happen from coming into the truth of our lives, as we understand it. We can always grow in our awareness and understanding of our experiences. As adoptees, we can look at our adoption story with expanded insight and curiosity, not just the version of our stories that might have been given to us by other people. Give yourself permission to speak, feel, and write your own truth, even if it doesn't fit with others' expectations or the habitual narratives, or versions of stories, that are well-worn paths.

There might be times of fantasy as an adoptee, imagining things that aren't true, but we might have wished them to be or imagined them to be, as we filled in various blanks or unknowns in our own stories.

It is common for adoptees to create versions of our origin stories and fantasize about who our biological parents might have been (unless you are part of an open adoption and have that information already), wondering if they were rich and famous, or in some way idealized human beings who would have given us perfect lives. Of course, we know that isn't true, but there is the possibility, if you wish, as an adoptee, to make up any version of our origin story we want, in the absence of the real story or facts about it.

Truth can refer to many things: the truth of who we are, the truth of our story as we know it, the truth of the facts of our origin story, the truths that we have been told. The truth as we want it to be.

The truth is...there can be many versions of it! It is common in a family for people to describe the same events with very different versions of the story, different versions of the truth. By nature, there is subjective reality to the truth of our lives.

JOURNALING PROMPTS

What truth have I always felt inside, even if no one else ever named it?

_____

_____

_____

_____

_____

_____

_____

_____

_____

_____

_____

_____

_____

_____

What parts of my story feel true to me, regardless of
what others have said?

_____

_____

_____

_____

_____

_____

_____

The truth I most needed to hear as a child was...

_____

_____

_____

_____

_____

_____

_____

_____

_____

_____

What does "living my truth" mean to me today?

_____

_____

_____

_____

_____

_____

_____

_____

_____

_____

FROM THE PAGES OF MY JOURNAL

When I was a young teenager and heard the song "Summer of '69" by Bryan Adams, I often imagined that he was my biological father, since I was conceived earlier that year. I later learned that he was only ten years old when I was born, a detail I never thought to consider in my fantasy and imagination about my biological roots. For a few years, it was a false truth I wanted to believe. Instead of wondering who my biological father might be, I just picked one. Even though I loved my dad completely, there was another dad I also wondered about. Both truths were true at the same time.

ROOTED

"Roots are not only in the past, they are also in the present, in the choices I make to belong to myself."

—LYNDA MONK

There are many metaphors used to talk about family, including family trees and family roots. With this is the idea that we are rooted in our families; they offer this place of belonging and identity, for better or for worse, depending on our circumstances. We also carry our roots inside of us, giving us this sense of being grounded, and planted in the gardens of our own lives. We create new roots too! Being rooted and grounded is not just about where we come from, it's about where we choose to stand.

JOURNALING PROMPTS

What are some of the roots I've created for myself?

_____

_____

_____

_____

_____

_____

_____

_____

What grounds me, or roots me, when I feel disconnected,
overwhelmed, or uncertain?

_____

_____

_____

_____

_____

_____

_____

_____

_____

_____

How do I know when I am taking a stand for the truth
of who I am?

_____

_____

_____

_____

_____

_____

_____

What core values help ground me in who I am and who I am becoming?

FROM THE PAGES OF MY JOURNAL

My parents didn't just raise me, they rooted me. I always felt like they were my "real parents," and I was their daughter. They never made me feel less-than, or borrowed; I always felt loved, like I belonged with them. I never referred to them as my "adoptive parents" or myself as their "adopted daughter." They are my parents, and I am their daughter. And still, I knew something was missing, because it was. Both things were true at the same time. These truths never were, and still aren't to this day, mutually exclusive. I belonged to them, and I also belonged to someone else. And what has truly rooted me in my life is knowing that I also belong to myself.

Pause & Reflect: Awareness to Action

As I reflect on the ROOTS section of this guide...

What do I notice?

How do I feel?

What insights am I having?

What action would I like to take based on the awareness I'm gaining?

What are my next steps, if any?

RECOGNITION
Acknowledging emotional impacts and processing

In the RECOGNITION section of this guide,
you are invited to explore:

- Acknowledge Complexity
- Core Wounds
- Connect with Emotion
- Grief & Loss
- Silence
- Shame
- Self-Worth

ACKNOWLEDGE COMPLEXITY

*"The human heart is big enough to hold multiple
truths at once. Love and loss. Peace and pain.
Gratitude and longing."*

—L. R. KNOST

Realizing that adoption isn't just a "happy ending" but
a layered experience that can include love, loss, grief,
confusion, belonging, searching for identity, and so much
more, is part of what opens a door to our expanded
awareness, healing, and resilience. There is no neat little
package that adoption wraps up in, nor is there a single right
way to think about it, feel about it, or live with it. Likewise,
there is no wrong way to try to understand it or integrate it
into our self-understanding and our overall life experience
as adoptees. By its very nature, adoption is complex and
involved. It is rarely straightforward; this is especially true
when it's unpacked and explored more fully. Adoption holds
many paradoxes and realities; it's like a puzzle with many
interlocking pieces.

JOURNALING PROMPTS

What are some parts of my adoption story that I've
found difficult to talk about or feel?

How has my identity been shaped by the presence of both gain and loss?

What's complicated, or feels complex, to me about being an adoptee?

_____

_____

_____

_____

_____

_____

_____

_____

_____

_____

_____

_____

_____

_____

_____

_____

_____

_____

_____

What's easy and straightforward, in my experience, about being an adoptee?

_____

_____

_____

_____

_____

_____

_____

_____

FROM THE PAGES OF MY JOURNAL

One of my dear friends once asked me why I want to write my adoptee memoir, with a tone that suggested what she was really wondering was, what is there to even write about? She also didn't seem to understand, and might have even been a bit judgmental, when she asked me why I wanted to find out more about my biological roots, like why wouldn't I just leave it alone, what difference does it make? She knows my family, she knows I was brought up in a loving home, and that I love my parents dearly, and it was hard for her to understand why any of the "adoption stuff" even mattered at all. I realized in that moment that there is so much complexity to being adopted and all the feelings and realities that can come with it that I didn't even really try to explain; I simply said, "it's complicated and it just matters to me."

CORE WOUNDS

"We are all many stories, some told, some hidden, all true."

—NIKITA GILL

There are lots of terms that get used in the adoption space about the nature of some of the core emotional wounds we might face as adoptees. These have been called primal wounds, abandonment wounds, rejection wounds, fear of abandonment wounds, pre-verbal trauma, attachment wounds, and so forth. It's important to realize that, just because we were adopted, that does not mean we are guaranteed to suffer from such emotional and psychological wounds. They aren't our fate or destiny; however, they are common and understandable wounds resulting from all that can be part of the very nature of what it means to be adopted and to be an adoptee.

I like to think of it like other psychological wounds that might be relevant for a given population of people. For example, many veterans who experienced war may suffer from PTSD (post-traumatic stress disorder) but it doesn't mean that all people who go to war will experience PTSD. It is a risk, not a guarantee. There are many mitigating and influential factors that impact the onset of such wounds.

The same is true for adoptees. The more support we have, the more ability we have to talk about, heal, and integrate our experiences as adoptees with trusted and skilled individuals who are kind and non-judgemental—people who are helpers, healers and listeners, people who understand the nature and risk of such wounds—the more we can mitigate the risk of suffering from them ourselves. We can also talk to ourselves through journaling, and this self-dialogue can also be healing, kind, and affirming.

JOURNALING PROMPTS

What does the word "wound" mean to me in the context of adoption?

Where do I notice pain or tenderness in my
adoptee story?

If my wound had a voice, what would it ask for? What would it need?

_____

_____

_____

_____

_____

_____

_____

_____

How has love helped me heal any core wounds I've experienced?

_____

_____

_____

_____

_____

_____

_____

FROM THE PAGES OF MY JOURNAL

I never thought I had a core adoption wound. Even when I read about things related to adoption, which I did in my twenties in my early social work career within child welfare, I never really thought it related to me, even though I was adopted. I was fine. I was happy. I was emotionally and psychologically well-adjusted.

One afternoon, when I went for a home visit to see one of my clients, I arrived at her place and she was very distraught. Almost before I got in the front door, she essentially tossed her three-month-old baby boy in my direction and, as I barely caught him in my arms, she begged me to take him home and be his mother, because she couldn't do it, and she didn't want to do it. She didn't want to be his mother. I was twenty-three at the time, just out of university with my social work degree, and as I held this woman's baby boy in my arms, soothing him while he cried and while she cried, I felt like crying too. I didn't cry in that moment rather, I dealt with the situation at hand as best I could, which involved getting her some crisis support and respite care for her baby boy.

But that night, when I went to bed, I cried. I cried and cried, and thought to myself, is this how it happened? Did my own birth mother just toss me into the arms of a random woman and ask her to be my mother instead of her?

This was long before I knew anything about the details of my own adoption. I felt a deep pain inside as I contemplated this possibility. In that moment, I encountered my own adoption wound. It was around that time I decided that I would do more to learn about my own origin and adoption story.

CONNECT WITH EMOTION

"As adoptees, our emotions can be like compasses that can lead us back to the parts of ourselves that we never want to lose."

—LYNDA MONK

A common expression in therapeutic language and in trauma-informed work is "to feel is to heal." As adoptees, we have a right to feel and embrace all of our emotions. Part of healing and growing as adoptees often includes exploring emotions that we might have suppressed, or not acknowledged or even recognized in our experiences.

There is a common expression attributed to Carl Jung, the founder of analytical psychology: "What we resist persists." In other words, when we avoid or deny difficult emotions or experiences, they tend to grow stronger and show up in other ways, which can include physically in our bodies, in our overall health, and in our relationships.

When we allow ourselves to identify, connect with, and feel our emotions, including sadness, anger, confusion, shame, and guilt, it can be so cathartic and freeing. We might even experience feelings of relief that bring a sense of release, lightness, and letting go. We can also connect with our joy, love, passion, gratitude, and vitality as adoptees. Our true healing and wholeness comes from awareness and acceptance of the breadth of our emotions.

Emotions are energy; they have a vibrational frequency to them. Our feelings are fluid and always changing. We are emotional beings, emotion moves through our body, and it is healthy to feel what we feel. Yet, sometimes, knowing what we feel can be challenging. We are so used to being asked things like "How are you?" and answering "Fine" that we might not even know how we feel about certain things at various times in our life. We can learn how to identify our emotions and expand our capacity to connect with them through journaling.

We learn a lot about emotion—in particular, whether or not it is okay to express our emotions—when we are children within our families. When I worked in children's mental health, it was often said by therapists that children can only learn to regulate the emotions they are "allowed" to have. Perhaps the same is true for adults, including for adoptees. Many adoptees only learn emotional regulation, and develop the ability to access and feel emotions, when caregivers, family, friends, or others encourage the expression of emotions in open and healthy ways. It's important to not dismiss adoptees' emotions or deny them, which can happen sometimes, even with well-meaning caregivers. We might even dismiss our own emotions sometimes.

Try to let yourself connect with your emotions with curiosity and interest, without any judgement of yourself or others. You might ask yourself, "I wonder how I feel about (this or that)?" Let curiosity be a gentle guide for exploring your feelings and for emotional self-expression. You can express your emotions through words, as well as non-verbally, for example through movement, art, and journaling.

JOURNALING PROMPTS

When I think about my adoption experience, what emotions are most familiar to me? Where do I feel these emotions in my body?

_____

_____

_____

_____

_____

_____

_____

_____

_____

_____

_____

_____

_____

_____

_____

_____

What emotions have I been holding back, or hiding,
around any part of my adoption story?

_____

_____

_____

_____

_____

_____

_____

Are there any emotions I've been told, directly or indirectly, that I'm "not allowed" to feel?

If my emotions could write a letter to me, what would they want me to know?

_____

_____

_____

_____

_____

_____

_____

_____

_____

_____

_____

_____

FROM THE PAGES OF MY JOURNAL

We didn't talk about being adopted when we were children in our family, beyond being told about it, and by extension, there was no acknowledgement that we might actually have any feelings about it or have any reason to have any feelings about it. It was simply a matter of fact. We were so young when we were told we were adopted, it was just sort of there in the background of life as a non-thing. Until I got older and it felt like a something.

GRIEF & LOSS

*"You are allowed to mourn the parts of your
adoptee story that no one else understands, the
parts that you might not even understand yourself.
Grief doesn't have to be justified."*

—LYNDA MONK

Grief and loss are common emotions for adoptees and others
in the adoption triangle, especially birth mothers. Whether
this grief is expressed or unexpressed, it is often in the lived
experience and quiet truths of adoption. Loss, and hence
grief, the emotion we feel when we have experienced loss,
can be felt at a very deep level.

It's not just possible "adoption wounds" and "abandonment
issues" that might cause grief as adoptees, but other losses
in life can feel extra challenging too—for example, when
we experience other life experiences, like losing someone
we love, death, betrayals, and abandonments. These sorts of
hurts and losses can cut a little deeper for adoptees. We might
feel triggered by these losses, or numb, or profoundly hurt.
Betrayals might feel unforgiveable because they consciously
or subconsciously trigger our original abandonment wound,
which might have felt like the first betrayal in our lives, even
if we understand why it happened or can intellectualize why
it happened. Losses can compound, and grief can feel intense.

There are many losses inherent to the adoption experience,
including the loss of our original family, loss of being raised
by our biological parents, loss of identity, loss of a coherent
narrative about our lives, loss of innocence, loss of trust, loss
of self-understanding—the list of losses can go on.

JOURNALING PROMPTS

How have I experienced grief in relation to being adopted?

_____

_____

_____

_____

_____

_____

_____

_____

_____

_____

_____

_____

_____

_____

_____

_____

_____

_____

_____

_____

What losses, both visible and invisible, have I
experienced as a result of being adopted?

_____

_____

_____

_____

_____

_____

_____

_____

_____

_____

_____

_____

Is there a loss I haven't allowed myself to fully
acknowledge or feel? What stops me from allowing my
grief and loss?

_____

_____

_____

_____

_____

_____

_____

_____

_____

How can I find a sense of comfort and support as it relates to naming and feeling any grief I may have?

_____

_____

_____

_____

_____

_____

FROM THE PAGES OF MY JOURNAL

I didn't even know I had grief as an adoptee, as I was just focused on being good and keeping everyone happy, so that my parents never regretted "choosing me" as their daughter. I think I somehow felt I had to earn the right to stay. I also didn't think I had the right to feel sad or to feel grief, or to feel anything as an adoptee, other than to feel grateful I was adopted in the first place.

SILENCE

"Silence is not empty; it is full of the unspoken, the unseen, and the felt."

—LYNDA MONK

In the world of adoption, silence is rarely empty. Instead, it is filled with the weight of what was never said, the questions left unanswered, and the stories waiting to be told. It is filled with what might have been. It is filled with what could not be said by birth parents (mostly birth mothers), adoptive parents, and our own empty places as adoptees.

Silence may be present in many parts of the adoption experience. There are silences around conception stories, pregnancy and birth stories, and relinquishment stories. Silences around origins, loss, identity, and emotion which are sometimes imposed, sometimes chosen, often complex.

Where there is silence, there is often secrecy and shame. Part of healing and growth can include breaking silences that are often better voiced. Silence can also be a quiet state we enter that feels good and nourishing, a place we can feel peaceful. Not something that is void, but a reservoir of quiet and calm that we can fill and replenish ourselves with.

JOURNALING PROMPTS

What silences existed around my adoption story growing up? Were there things people didn't talk about or told me not to talk about?

How did these silences, if there were any, impact me?

What silences am I willing to give voice to now?

How can silence be a comfort at times?

_____

_____

_____

_____

_____

_____

_____

_____

_____

_____

_____

FROM THE PAGES OF MY JOURNAL

*I lived in my birth mother's silence for decades. I was my
birth mother's best-kept secret. Her father didn't know
she had a child, I would have been his first granddaughter,
her six siblings never knew she had a child, her husband
of twenty-two-plus years never knew she had a child. Only
her mother knew that I was born and then relinquished for
adoption, I suppose in that way I was also one of her best-
kept secrets too. Being told I was adopted was also the
first secret I was asked to keep as a little girl. Silence and
secrecy were a common voice in my adoption experience,
until they weren't and I started asking questions.*

SHAME

"Shame is the intensely painful feeling or experience of believing that we are flawed and therefore unworthy of love and belonging."

—BRENÉ BROWN

I love the work of Brené Brown, a social worker, researcher, and bestselling author in the areas of shame and vulnerability. She teaches that shame makes us feel that something is wrong with who we are, not just what we've done. It can make us feel isolated and diminished. It thrives in secrecy, silence, and judgement. The antidote to shame is empathy. Her work is not with adoptees specifically, and shame can be a part of our shared human experience. However, given the complexities of adoption and its inherent relationship with issues of identity, belonging, and attachment, shame can be a common emotion that adoptees feel and struggle with at times, feeling unworthy of love and belonging. We are absolutely worthy of these things!

Just thinking about and writing about shame can be a vulnerable thing to do. As Brené Brown says, when we can be vulnerable, we can reduce and even eliminate feelings of shame. Shame can't survive in the presence of empathy, self-compassion, and connection. Seek connection and care with people who know your worth!

JOURNALING PROMPTS

What would I say to a younger version of myself who might have felt shame for being adopted?

What helps me feel safe enough to be real and vulnerable?

What truth would I like to speak that shame has tried to silence?

Who in my life offers me connection, care, empathy, and/
or compassion?

SELF-WORTH

"Worthy isn't something you become. It's something you remember."

—NAYYIRAH WAHEED

The core wound of abandonment that is part of an adoptee's experience can create a sense of self-doubt about one's worth. Even in loving homes, adoptees may carry a deep sense of loss from being separated from biological mothers and their original family, whether that is in conscious awareness or not. This could lead to unconscious beliefs like, "If I was given up, maybe I wasn't worthy of being kept, maybe I wasn't worthy of being loved."

There is value in feeling worthy because it allows you to accept yourself as you are, rather than constantly striving to earn approval from others. It also reduces internal self-criticism or negative self-talk, and creates greater feelings of self-kindness.

JOURNALING PROMPTS

What does *being worthy just because I exist* mean to me?

_____

_____

_____

_____

_____

_____

How can I release the idea that I must prove or earn
my worth?

_____

_____

_____

_____

_____

_____

_____

_____

When have I truly felt seen and accepted as worthy by
myself or someone else?

_____

_____

_____

_____

_____

How do I define my worth today, in my own words?

_____

_____

_____

_____

_____

_____

_____

FROM THE PAGES OF MY JOURNAL

*I have always had a good sense of self-worth. I feel
confident. I feel like I am enough. However, sometimes
I felt like I was too much for my mom. She would often
shush me, or tell me to not "get too big for my britches"
when I would share some of my life dreams with her. She
would also silence me when my curiosity about people and
life entered conversations. I would ask people questions
about themselves; my mom would always get me to stop
and say it is none of my business. I often felt like I was
too much for her. She didn't like to ask other people
questions but always stayed in the land of small talk and
what neighbour was doing what, looking out the front
window of our house speculating on where someone was
going when they backed out of their driveway. I didn't care
where they were going, it was none of my business and it
didn't interest me in the least.*

*I wanted to learn the inner thoughts of people, what
made them tick. I wanted to talk about ideas. I wanted to
hear people's stories. I felt embarrassed and ashamed
at times, just being myself, because I felt like there was
something wrong with me for caring about these things
since they were supposed to be "none of my business."
Perhaps that is why I chose a career where speaking with,
and listening to, others was the heart of my helping work.*

*When I met my birth mother, she would dive right into
meaningful questions, saying she hates small talk. I felt
validated and like I instantly understood where this part
of me came from.*

Pause & Reflect: Awareness to Action

As I reflect on the RECOGNITION section of this guide...

What do I notice?

How do I feel?

What insights am I having?

What action would I like to take based on the awareness I'm gaining?

What are my next steps, if any?

RESILIENCE
Connecting with inner strength

In the RESILIENCE section of this guide, you
are invited to explore:

- Thriving & Resilience
- Trauma
- Addiction
- Safety & Security
- Fear of Abandonment
- Choice
- Embodiment

THRIVING & RESILIENCE

"Resilience is a dance, not a stance."

—DANIELLE LAPORTE

Thriving and resilience are common words used in personal growth, change management, health and wellness, leadership, education, and other fields that care to refer to what helps people do and be their best, and what helps people cope and be strong under pressure and during times of change.

I have taught workshops on these topics for years, as I've always been interested in what it takes to truly thrive in life, and with that, what does thriving even mean? To thrive is another one of these subjective ideas like healing and growth. You could ask ten people how they would define thriving, and you will get ten different answers.

According to common definitions of resilience, it means our ability to bounce back after adverse situations while remaining high-functioning and productive. Most people think of it as our inner strength and our ability to cope during difficult times. It is sometimes referred to as our ability to bend and not break.

As adoptees, we don't always have to be strong to thrive and be resilient. We can just be human too. We can thrive on our own terms. I believe thriving is about our ability to grow, heal, and achieve more than what is defined by our circumstances alone. Thriving is about knowing ourselves, believing in ourselves, caring for ourselves, and enjoying life to the fullest in the best ways we can!

JOURNALING PROMPTS

What is one challenge I have faced as an adoptee that I
have grown through?

_____

_____

_____

_____

_____

_____

_____

_____

What strengths did I discover about myself?

_____

_____

_____

_____

_____

_____

_____

_____

_____

What is something I've overcome that reminds me of my inner strength and light?

_____

_____

_____

_____

_____

_____

_____

What would I like to acknowledge or appreciate about my own resilience?

_____

_____

_____

_____

_____

_____

_____

_____

What does "thriving on your own terms" mean to me?

FROM THE PAGES OF MY JOURNAL

I'm a resilient person. I know that. I've been through enough things, and witnessed enough other people go through challenging times, that I know I have a lot of inner strength. I know I can bounce back from times of high stress and difficult situations. I know I can stay sane when the world feels crazy. I know I have many good and healthy coping skills, tools, and supports for dealing with what life throws my way. I know I have an optimistic, hopeful, flexible, and positive outlook on life. Research by Linda Hoopes, who I trained with, and others in the resiliency field, teaches that these characteristics are foundations to our resilience. The truth is, I'm so good at being strong that what my resilience might need most of all is to take a break from being strong, positive, and productive all the time, and just simply rest. I can thrive in stillness too. I can thrive by being tender with myself. I can thrive with balance between giving and receiving. I can thrive sitting in the garden watching our beautiful flowers grow. I can thrive by living my best life, one day at a time.

TRAUMA

"Trauma is not what happens to you. Trauma is what happens inside you as a result of what happens to you."

—DR. GABOR MATÉ

Adoption is often considered a form of trauma, especially from a psychological and developmental perspective. Trauma is a vast topic, and I won't presume to do it justice in only a few short paragraphs. There are many individuals who do excellent work in this area. Experts Dr. Gabor Maté, Dr. Bessel van der Kolk, and Dr. Peter Levine are among my favorite authors to read, listen to, and learn from.

Trauma is the Greek word for wound. Trauma is the wound itself, which may manifest as anxiety, or having a negative worldview, or heightened startle reflexes, or beliefs of not being wanted or loved, etc. Dr. Gabor Maté, and others, explain that there are many symptoms that can be part of the wound of trauma. The trauma-inducing event is different than the actual trauma wound itself. For example, being adopted can be a trauma-inducing event that might lead to a wound (trauma), and adaptations may get made to try to cope with this painful wound.

While not all adoptees will describe their experience as traumatic, it's important to understand that many adoptees do carry wounds. There are different types of traumas related to adoption that can include relinquishment trauma, and pre-verbal separation trauma, and attachment traumas. Also, some adoptees experience other trauma-inducing events, like abuse or further rejection or isolation, in their adoptive families. Some families can be safer, healthier, and more loving than others, and that's true of adoptive families too.

JOURNALING PROMPTS

What helps me feel safe and grounded in my body
right now?

_____

_____

_____

_____

_____

_____

_____

_____

What wounds do I carry from my adoptee experience?

_____

_____

_____

_____

_____

_____

_____

_____

When I start to feel overwhelmed, what are a few small things I can do to comfort myself?

_____

_____

_____

_____

_____

_____

What is an affirmation that can bring feelings of comfort and calm? For example, I am safe in this moment. I can slow down. I don't have to rush my healing. I'm okay. I've got this. I am fully present in this moment. Breathe.

_____

_____

_____

_____

_____

_____

_____

_____

ADDICTION

*"Addiction is often the language of
unacknowledged grief."*

—DR. GABOR MATÉ

There are studies that recognize an increased risk of addiction among adoptees. Research shows that addiction and substance use disorders are more prevalent among adoptees than in the general population. For example, one study (in the *Journal of the American Academy of Child & Adolescent Psychiatry*) showed that adoptees are two to four times more likely to struggle with substance abuse than non-adoptees. The elevated risk applies across age groups from adolescence into adulthood.

Addiction can be a way we try to fill empty places. Addiction can also be genetic, a disease, a decision, or a series of poor choices that get out of control. It is something that can emerge in efforts to self-medicate unbearable emotional, psychological, and/or physical pain.

There are many types of addictions, including substance addictions, which can include physical dependence on alcohol, drugs, and other substances. There are also behavioral addiction to things like gambling, sex, pornography, shopping/spending, gaming, work ("workaholism"), food, excessive exercise, and so forth. There are also emotional or psychological addictions, such as addiction to drama or chaos, addiction to approval or validation, codependency (being addicted to helping or fixing others), adrenaline or crisis cycles, addiction to perfectionism, addiction to suffering or victimhood as a familiar identity.

As Dr. Gabor Maté says, "The question is not why the addiction, but why the pain?" He teaches that many addictions are not about the substance or behaviour itself, but about the underlying pain, trauma, disconnection, or unmet need.

It's important to note that having an increased risk of addictions as an adoptee does not mean it is our destiny. Meaningful connections, self-awareness, and therapy are powerful tools for prevention and healing, and can help mitigate the risk of addictions and other challenges adoptees might face.

JOURNALING PROMPTS

What role has pain or emotional discomfort played in my relationship with addictive behaviors or coping mechanisms?

Are there particular emotions or memories I try to numb, avoid, or escape from? When do these patterns tend to show up?

What unmet needs might I be trying to soothe or fill through this behavior?

What healthier ways of coping would I like to explore or cultivate?

How can I offer compassion to the part of me that developed this coping mechanism?

SAFETY & SECURITY

"Safety is the soil from which our healing grows."

—LYNDA MONK

In my early social work training, we were taught about psychologist Abraham Maslow's hierarchy of needs. It suggests that we must have basic survival needs met, followed by safety needs, including security, stability, and protection, before we can have self-actualization needs, such as our personal growth and purpose, fulfilled. So, in many ways, part of our growth as adoptees requires that we find our ways to feel safe and secure, not under threat of being harmed or abandoned. When we feel safe, including emotionally safe, we can relax enough to reflect and explore, and integrate our experiences and our emotions, and this can lead to our healing and growth. Only you know what you need to feel emotionally safe and secure, and these are important needs to nurture, protect, and honor. I once heard someone say, "It's wise to choose inner feelings of safety over outer approval from others." I like this wisdom!

JOURNALING PROMPTS

What does emotional safety feel like in my body?

_____

_____

_____

_____

_____

_____

In what ways did I learn to protect myself emotionally, and perhaps physically too, as a child?

What people or places have helped me feel safe, accepted, and grounded in my life?

_____

_____

_____

_____

What boundaries and practices help me feel safe in
my life now?

_____

_____

_____

_____

_____

_____

_____

_____

_____

_____

_____

FROM THE PAGES OF MY JOURNAL

*When I was in the second grade, I disclosed to the whole
class that I was adopted. I wasn't the only one; Chuck and*

Jason also raised their hands to answer the teacher's question, "Who here is adopted?" It was part of a series of questions she was posing to all of us seven-year-olds. Who likes dogs? Who has been on airplane? Who is adopted? That kind of thing.

In the days and weeks after I disclosed this secret that I had been asked to keep by my parents, and I got over my extreme emotional upset that followed this spontaneous disclosure, a boy in my class, who shall remain nameless, would often tease and taunt me by saying, "Your real mom is going to come back and steal you away from your parents."

When I would resist and say, "That won't happen," he would just push and push and insist it was so. He'd continue and say she would come and climb up to the window of my bedroom and take me away and no one would know what happened or where I had gone. This threat terrified me!

I started to grow fearful of falling asleep. I would leave my room and try to crawl into bed with my parents, whose bedroom was across the hall from mine. They would always take me back to my room and put me in my own bed. One night, my dad asked what was wrong, why didn't I want to sleep in my own bed? I burst into tears and said, "Because she is going to come and take me away!"

He asked, "Who is going to come and take you away?"

"The other mommy who had me in her tummy," I told him, through choking sobs. I told him the whole story. He put his arms around me, and he reassured me that could never happen. I didn't fully believe him, but I did feel relief that I had told him. The next day, my dad drove me to school and said he wanted to talk to my teacher and to my classmate who was taunting me with this threat. I don't know what my dad ever said to my teacher or that boy, but all I know is, he never taunted me again. It took me a long, long time to feel safe and secure and truly believe that "she" wasn't going to come and take me away from my family.

FEAR OF ABANDONMENT

"Fear of abandonment isn't a flaw or a personal failing; it's an understandable response to the emotional wound of being left."

—LYNDA MONK

There are themes that can emerge for adoptees in relationships, that are true for all human beings. But there are some common themes that adoptees might face or experience. Adoptees may fear abandonment, or have a hard time letting go, or have a difficult time making attachment bonds in the first place. An "abandonment wound" may get triggered as we love others, and fear losing them or being left by them. This can happen without us even knowing or realizing we have an "abandonment wound" as adoptees.

The wound of abandonment is not your fault. This wound may always be a part of your story, but it doesn't have to control your life or your happiness. You can carry this past without it carrying you; you have the strength to heal this wound.

JOURNALING PROMPTS

What am I aware of that relates to the idea of an "abandonment wound?"

How do I relate to commitment and trust in relationships?

What things do I do, for better or for worse, to protect my heart from feelings of abandonment?

What parts of myself, if any, have I abandoned to feel safe or accepted by others?

What do I need right now to feel emotionally held and supported?

CHOICE

"In the space between stimulus and response, there is a space. In that space is our power to choose our response. In our response lies our growth and our freedom."

—VIKTOR E. FRANKL

Even if adoption is a loving choice, an adoptee might still feel unwanted or left behind or given away or not loveable. There are times when adoption was not a loving choice, it was a desperate choice. Or it may not have been a direct choice at all. For example, a child may have been apprehended from their parent(s) in child welfare systems or criminal justice systems or church systems, and so on. There may have been a biological parent who was unable to care for their own children and grandparents, or siblings, or aunties, or other family members might step up and become the legal guardians and adoptive parents in such situations. Many people can be making many choices in any single adoption story. There may be children who are already older when they are adopted, and they can have early childhood memories of their life and family experiences before being adopted.

The adoption space is full of conversations and literature and poems about "choice." It is almost a haunting word, hollow in some way. I believe so much about adoption is filled with choiceless choices, like giving up a baby in the first place was for many birth mothers in the era I was born in.

As adoptees, unless we have the details of our adoptions and why we were relinquished, and even if we do have these stories, we might lie awake at night wondering about choices that impacted our lives: "Why did my birth mother choose to give me away?" or "Why couldn't she choose to keep me?" or "Did her choice make me better off?" or "Did she even have a choice?" There are more questions than answers about choices, and that perhaps is true throughout all of our lives.

Our questions as adoptees will be shaped and influenced by the circumstances of our unique adoption experience. One young woman I supported, who was placed for adoption later in her childhood, wondered why her mother couldn't stop doing drugs so she could be her mother. Part of her knew it wasn't that simple; the other part of her felt that her mom was choosing drugs over her.

Our lives are shaped by choices: the choices other people make, and the choices we make! Even the seemingly choiceless choices we might make are still our choices. With choices, often, come questions, including unanswered questions about what might have been.

JOURNALING PROMPTS

What choices were made on my behalf before I had a voice? How do those choices live in me today?

What choices have other people made that have had a direct impact on me?

_____

_____

_____

_____

_____

What choices have I made in my life that I feel have been influenced or shaped by being an adoptee?

_____

_____

_____

_____

_____

_____

As I continue to grow on my adoptee journey, what choices feel important to me now? What new choices would I like to make in my life at this time?

_____

_____

_____

_____

_____

_____

_____

_____

_____

FROM THE PAGES OF MY JOURNAL

I always assumed, because it felt better that way in the absence of having any information, that my birth mother probably loved me and didn't have a choice but to place me up for adoption. That version of the story felt the easiest to hold.

When I met my birth mother at the age of thirty, I learned, thankfully, that version of the story was true. She did love me, she wished she could have kept me as her own, and that wasn't an option. She was an eighteen-year-old unwed Catholic girl in 1969, and her fate was sealed. When she told her mom she was pregnant, she was sent away to live with a priest's parents, and later to a "home for girls like her." She made the choiceless choice to give me up for adoption.

I've made the choice to bring compassion and love to my birth mother and to try my best to understand what it must have been like for her to have to relinquish me, her baby girl, for adoption. I think it broke her heart. And, even though I was only five days old when she handed me over to a social worker, long before my conscious memories could form, I think on a deep cellular level, it broke my heart too. This primal wound of severing is perhaps what quietly gets felt in me, even now, even though for most of my life, I have barely acknowledged it as a wound at all.

EMBODIMENT

"The body keeps the score."

—DR. BESSEL VAN DER KOLK

What does it mean to be embodied? To be embodied is to be fully present and connected to your body, experiencing life not just through thoughts and emotions, but also through physical sensation, awareness, and presence. It means not just living in our heads, but being attuned to what our bodies are communicating.

Dr. Bessel van der Kolk, a psychiatrist who has spent his career studying how children and adults adapt to traumatic experiences, has looked at neuroscience and attachment research, and he teaches the importance of somatic ways of healing. He teaches that the impact of trauma is upon the survival or animal part of the brain, and that some of the healing needed can happen through reconnecting with the body in safe and self-aware ways.

This matters because situations that have caused us emotional, psychological, and even physical wounds can be long gone, but the emotion can still be stuck in our body. Healing, wholeness, and integration can happen by getting emotion to flow, and that can happen by moving the body. By moving, releasing and expressing through the body, we can balance and release energy (emotion), making our body feel lighter and freer, and this frees and lightens our minds and hearts too. In the words of the late Gabrielle Roth, founder of the 5Rhythms® movement meditation practice in the late 1970s, "movement is medicine."

I have trained in Reiki (an energy healing modality), Healing Touch, and Esalen Massage. I have always been interested in a holistic understanding of healing mind, body, heart, and spirt. I value body-centered approaches to healing and living. I also believe talk therapy, a common modality for healing trauma, might not always be as helpful for adoptees because so often the trauma or early wounding might have happened during a pre-verbal stage of development, as babies. I'm not saying talk therapy isn't valuable, but I am saying I think there is huge value in holistic, embodied ways of healing and wholeness. These approaches focus on integrating the body, mind, and emotions, not just talking through experiences, but feeling and moving through them. For adoptees, or anyone working through trauma wounds, this can be especially powerful. We can't just intellectualize healing; ideally, we must embody it, because, as Dr. Bessel van der Kolk said, "The body keeps the score."

JOURNALING PROMPTS

What sensations do I notice in my body right now, without needing to change them?

Are there places in my body where I often feel tension, tightness, or numbness? What might those places be trying to tell me?

_____

_____

_____

_____

_____

_____

What does my body need more of right now? Rest, movement, touch, stillness, nourishment, etc.?

_____

_____

_____

_____

_____

_____

What does "being at home in my body" mean to me?

_____

_____

_____

_____

_____

_____

_____

_____

_____

_____

_____

FROM THE PAGES OF MY JOURNAL

When I move, when I dance 5Rhythms®, when I walk along the beach, when I do yoga in our living room, when I receive massage, when I sing loudly driving in the car alone, when I take a bubble bath, when I wear dresses that touch my skin at the knee, when I run or go to the gym, or do Bellyfit, or walk barefoot in the grass, or hike at Burgoyne Bay, or when I do tapping or EFT (emotional freedom technique), or meditate, or eat delicious food by candlelight, when I make love...when I remember my body and my senses, I am fully alive in the here and now. I am all of me, not just part of me. I am happy when I remember my body, when I nourish my senses, and honor my sensuality. I am happy in my own skin when I remember my aliveness in the moment. If my body is keeping score, I want it to have a high score of as many good things it can experience in this lifetime.

Pause & Reflect: Awareness to Action

As I reflect on the RESILIENCE section of this guide...

What do I notice?

How do I feel?

What insights am I having?

What action would I like to take based on the awareness I'm gaining?

What are my next steps, if any?

RELATIONSHIPS
Building meaningful connections and understanding attachment

In the RELATIONSHIPS section of this guide,
you are invited to explore:

- Family
- Nature & Nurture
- Attachment
- Intimate Relationships
- Culture & Ancestry
- Chosen Kin
- Trust

FAMILY

*"Family is made up of more than bloodlines, it is also
made of love lines."*

—LYNDA MONK

Our adoption stories, by their very nature, mean that we have
more than one family, whether we ever meet them or know
them or not.

Even if we never meet, search for, or have any awareness of
our original family, at the very least, if we know we are an
adoptee, we know there was a set of biological parents from
which we were conceived and born. There is an original
family that contributes to our genetics and ancestry. I have
grown a strong appreciation that my family is made of both
bloodlines and love lines, and these are equally strong threads
to be tethered to.

Among the things that make families strong are the stories,
moments, and memories shared together. The shared
experiences in life create our bonds and feelings of belonging.
Biological family is also very important as it is literally the
genetic material of who we are. Even if we never played cards
together, or went on family holidays, this "family" is there all
along too, in some more-than-skin-deep way.

JOURNALING PROMPTS

What does the word family mean to me today?

How has my definition of family changed over time?

What kinds of family relationships nourish me now?

_____
_____
_____
_____
_____
_____
_____
_____
_____

What kind of family energy or love am I calling into my
life moving forward?

_____
_____
_____
_____
_____
_____
_____
_____
_____

_____

_____

_____

_____

_____

_____

_____

FROM THE PAGES OF MY JOURNAL

When I was a young girl, I remember crying myself to sleep one night. I was crying because I felt so grateful for my parents and my family. I also felt deeply sad that there was another family out there that I also belonged to, even if they were strangers. I felt a sense of grief that I did not know who these people were, the people that I come from, the people I am made of. It felt so confusing because I would never want to be apart from my family, because I am made from them too. I am who I am in part because of the presence of their love throughout every day of my life. They are the people I've shared my life with, who I'm attached to and bonded with through shared memories and years of loving together. Yet, I also felt a bond for this invisible thread that had me silently connected to my original family too. I felt guilty for wanting to find them. I also felt scared that I wouldn't ever meet them. A part of me always felt like I existed in the space between two families, even though one of them was unknown to me. Even though I was deeply loved, protected, and cared for in the family that made me their own.

NATURE & NURTURE

"Nature provides potential; nurture unlocks it."

—STEVEN PINKER

Nature and nurture, nature versus nurture: These are aspects of who we are that have been explored deeply in many professional fields, including psychology, behavioral genetics, epigenetics, neuroscience, sociology, anthropology, social work, and counselling. In my early social work career, I often worked with individuals to understand how early environments (nurture) and family history (nature) impacted their current circumstances, including their emotional well-being. This can be especially important to consider in adoption and trauma healing. Nature includes our origins, biology, and innate traits. Nurture includes our upbringing, environment, and care.

In adoption, nature versus nurture acknowledges that, while adopted children inherit genetic traits from our biological parents, our upbringing and experiences within our adoptive family also play a crucial role in shaping, or at least influencing, who we become. Adoption lives at the intersection of nature and nurture.

JOURNALING PROMPTS

What parts of me feel like they've always been there regardless of who raised me?

_____

_____

_____

_____

What parts of my identity feel connected to something older or deeper than my lived experience?

In what ways did my environment influence who I've become?

What wisdom or power can I reclaim by honoring both where I come from and who I've chosen to become?

FROM THE PAGES OF MY JOURNAL

When I was a teenager I had a boyfriend, Mike, whose dad was a race car driver. We would go to the Delaware racetrack on Friday night and his dad would let us come down into the pit, where all the race cars and drivers were on the field inside the oval track. He even let me drive the car around the track one time on my own, after the races for the night were all finished. I was about fourteen and didn't have a driver's license. I loved it! Then and there, I wanted to become a female stock car racer. I told my parents about my newfound dream. My dad shook his head and laughed, and asked me, "Where is this crazy idea coming from?" I said, "I don't know, it just feels exciting when I'm at the racetrack, I really love it there. It's so much fun!"

Neither of my parents liked race cars, and they certainly were not keen on me driving one. They thought it was too dangerous, and overall a very bad idea. I decided they were probably right, it was a crazy and bad idea.

A couple of years ago, through the help of my dear friend Chris and Ancestry.com, I was so excited to learn the identity of my biological father. I sadly learned that he died in 2015; however, I discovered I have three half-siblings. I was elated to meet my two half-brothers, Chad and Ryan, and in the early stories that flowed, along with photos of my biological father, Rob Fletcher, I immediately got chills when they handed me a picture of him in full gear in his race car! I learned he was a passionate race car driver who won many races. Not just any races, but races at the very racetrack in Delaware, Ontario, where I often went on Friday nights as a teenage girl. Not only were the degrees of separation between us so slim, but I immediately knew where my desire for race car driving came from!

I so wish I could have told my parents this story, as I could have answered their question about where my crazy idea to become a stock car racer had come from.

ATTACHMENT

"Awareness of your attachment patterns is the first step to building the secure connections you've always deserved."

—DR. SUE JOHNSON

Attachment bonds are the emotional glue that connects one person to another, especially in close relationships. They are built through consistent, loving, and responsive caregiving over time. These bonds become the bedrock for how we understand love, trust, closeness, and our self-worth.

In addition to attachment bonds, we all have attachment styles that are born of the type of bonds and early caregiving we received. One can have a "secure attachment" style that includes feeling comfortable with closeness and independence. This often includes having a strong core belief of "I am worthy of love, and others can be trusted." This results from having consistent, loving care as a child. "Anxious attachment" style craves closeness, but fears abandonment, and may worry about being rejected or being "too much." This often stems from inconsistent caregiving. The "avoidant/dismissive attachment" style values independence and may avoid emotional intimacy, believing "I can only rely on myself." With this style, a person might downplay their need for connection, and it often results from emotional needs being ignored. Last is "disorganized (fearful-avoidant) attachment," where the person may experience intense emotional swings in relationships, wanting connection but fearing being hurt. The belief can be "I want closeness, but it's dangerous." This attachment style is often linked to trauma, loss, or having caregivers who were frightening or unpredictable.

Many adoptees experience early disruption in attachment, such as separation from a birth parent or early neglect. These experiences can lead to insecure attachment patterns, including anxious, avoidant, and disorganized styles. It is so important to know that healing is always possible. Safe and loving relationships can help reshape attachment patterns over time. Our attachment style is not a conclusion, it's a starting point for understanding, healing, and choosing new ways to connect that can help us have the types of relationships we need and want, not just as adoptees, but as individuals having a wide range of relationship experiences.

JOURNALING PROMPTS

How was love shown to me as a child by my caregivers?

How do I tend to respond when someone gets emotionally close to me?

In what ways, if any, do I try to protect myself in relationships?

_____

_____

_____

_____

_____

_____

Who are the people in my life today that I have emotionally safe and caring attachments with?

_____

_____

_____

_____

_____

_____

_____

_____

_____

_____

_____

_____

INTIMATE RELATIONSHIPS

"To be fully seen by somebody, then, and be loved anyhow—this is a human offering that can border on miraculous."

—ELIZABETH GILBERT

For many adoptees, intimacy is where the echo of early separation is felt most deeply. Intimate relationships can be the place where the fear of loss, the need for closeness, and the longing to be fully known and loved unconditionally all meet. Intimate relationships are vulnerable relationships. They are open-hearted spaces where we get naked, literally. As C .S. Lewis wrote, "To love at all is to be vulnerable. Love anything and your heart will be wrung and possibly broken."

Healthy intimacy requires showing up and being brave. I believe adoptees know how to be brave and take risks with love! We may have also learned to protect our hearts. Intimate relationships can be rich places filled with potential for expanded healing and growth.

JOURNALING PROMPTS

How do I tend to show up in close intimate relationships?

_____

_____

_____

_____

_____

_____

_____

What fears do I carry in intimate relationships?

_____

_____

_____

_____

_____

_____

In what ways can I be more honest or vulnerable in a
relationship with myself and with others?

_____

_____

_____

_____

_____

_____

_____

_____

_____

_____

What do I want and deserve in a deeply connected, intimate relationship?

_____

_____

_____

_____

_____

_____

_____

_____

_____

FROM THE PAGES OF MY JOURNAL

The two greatest places I have learned the healing power of love, the places I have been stretched and grown the most, in my heart and as a person, have been in my intimate relationships and being a mother to our two sons. Wherever I have loved the most, have also been the circumstances in which I have grown the most. I would not be who I am today without wholeheartedly, and courageously, saying yes to love! Not just once, but every single day. Being emotionally naked is often exhilarating and terrifying all at once. In my marriage, where I am truly loved, it is the softest, most beautiful imperfect fully human place for my heart to land.

CULTURE & ANCESTRY

"Knowing your history gives you a sense of strength and purpose."

—MAYA ANGELOU

Ancestry often represents more than just DNA, it also symbolizes origin, continuity, and belonging. Maybe that is why it is often quite instinctual for adoptees to yearn to know where we come from. It is not just adoptees who can long to reclaim or reconnect with lost culture, heritage, ancestry or history. Anyone who has, for any reason, been separated from their culture and ancestry can feel the primal pull back to their roots.

Many adoptees grow up in families and communities that do not reflect their birth culture, race, or ancestry. This can lead to a sense of cultural loss, a feeling of disconnection from ancestral roots, and feeling caught between two worlds, the family you were raised with and the one you came from. There can be very painful stories when people have been taken from their culture, especially with no choice of their own.

I want to acknowledge Canada's Indigenous people, many of whom have very traumatic and painful losses as a result of such experiences, being taken and placed in residential schools, and to this day being overrepresented in our foster care system. While this is beyond the scope of this book, their history and experiences are in my mind and heart as I write this. This sad reality plays out with children being separated from their culture, families, and places of belonging, in a variety of ways, in many countries around the globe.

Many countries have what is referred to as customary care. For example, in Canada, this is a traditional system of care for First Nations, Inuit, and Métis children, involving placement with a non-parent caregiver according to the child's community's customs, aiming to maintain cultural identity, values, practices, and family connections.

Exploring culture and ancestry can be a healing and empowering journey. Some adoptees learn about their heritage, travel to ancestral lands, or connect with biological family members. It also can be meaningful to create rituals to honor lineage that an adoptee didn't get to know intimately. Even though a person wasn't raised in their birth culture, they carry it in their bones. We are descendants of our culture and ancestry in spirit and in story.

JOURNALING PROMPTS

In what ways do I feel connected, or disconnected, from my culture of origin?

If I could speak to my ancestors, what questions
would I ask?

_____

_____

_____

_____

_____

_____

_____

_____

_____

_____

Are there aspects of culture or ancestry I'd like to
reclaim or redefine for myself?

_____

_____

_____

_____

_____

_____

_____

_____

What parts of my adoptive culture have shaped me?

CHOSEN KIN

"In the tapestry of life, chosen kin are the golden threads—placed with intention, woven with love."

—L. M. MONTGOMERY

We can choose who we love. We can choose family. Many people will say their chosen kin are their true kin. With adoption, that is the language often used: "You were chosen." This, of course, is a different reference than what is commonly referred to as chosen kin. The key difference is that we did not choose to be adopted, others chose. Our birth parents chose to relinquish us for adoption, or the choice was made for them. Our adoptive parents chose to adopt us. But we did not choose to be adoptees.

Chosen kin are the people you choose to hold close, people who feel like family by love rather than blood or legal ties. As adoptees, we may have chosen kin in the circle of people we have made a connection with, who we trust, and love, and are committed to showing up for in life. There is an expression that says, "Chosen kin are the best family because you get to choose them."

JOURNALING PROMPTS

What is your experience with chosen kin?

How does chosen kin feel different, or similar, to
biological or adoptive family?

What emotional needs do my chosen kin help meet that may not have been fully met in my adoptive family or family of origin?

_____

_____

_____

_____

_____

_____

_____

_____

_____

_____

_____

_____

_____

_____

_____

_____

_____

_____

What are some small ways my chosen kin make me feel at home in myself?

_____

_____

_____

_____

_____

_____

_____

FROM THE PAGES OF MY JOURNAL

Some of my dearest friends are also my chosen kin, people I think of as family. People I will love and care for all my life. I am an auntie to some of my best friends' children, and I have loved these kids all their lives. They are all adults now and, even if we don't talk often, I love them each day and that is felt whether we are together or apart. I have also witnessed my sons with chosen kin, a couple who have loved them all their lives, who were originally our neighbours and helped with early caregiving of our sons. To this day, our boys have special bonds with Jennifer and Josh, and they share meals together, and go on adventures. Our boys know they could turn to them for help with anything at any time and they will be there for them. It's so special and I'm so grateful for the love they/ we share together. They are chosen kin.

TRUST

"Trust yourself. You know more than you think you do."

—BENJAMIN SPOCK

There are many ingredients needed to create and sustain healthy relationships with family, intimate partners, friends, chosen kin, and others who matter to us. Trust and all that goes with it, including things like reliability, honesty, safety, boundaries, and vulnerability, are what allow for deeper and more meaningful connections. Trust grows in emotionally safe spaces. Trust can be hard at times for lots of reasons; the primary one is that it has been broken.

Some adoptees have difficulty with trusting others. Some adoptees find it hard to trust themselves. It matters to trust our own instincts, emotions, and bodies. We can strengthen our relationship with self-trust by honoring our intuition and listening to our wise inner voice.

We can do this with the help of self-reflective practices and tools like journaling, including with this guided journal. Writing helps give language to trust and vulnerability, it gives voice to who we are, what we think, what we feel, and what we need.

JOURNALING PROMPTS

What's one way I trusted today?

What are high-trust behaviours that I value in myself and others? (i.e. honesty, reliability, respect, do what they say they are going to do, etc.)

How do I know when I'm betraying myself or not honoring my inner truth?

_____

_____

_____

_____

_____

When have I listened to my intuition or instincts, and it served me well?

_____

_____

_____

_____

_____

_____

_____

_____

FROM THE PAGES OF MY JOURNAL

My dad used to always say, "Trust is earned, not just given."

I've always said, "I'll trust you until you give me a reason not to."

Trust can take time to build, and it can be lost in an instant. It's always a worthy pursuit since so much is lost, or not possible in the first place, without it. Maybe everything!

I value trust not because I am an adoptee, but because I want to live with integrity and want the people I choose to love and spend my time and life with to do the same. As a mom, I've always said to my boys that honesty is a core value I have, and I hope in our relationship together they can honor it, and I will do the same. And we do. I know, it is the foundation for our rich relationships together, filled with open communication, respect, trust, and deep love. I respect my boys as they have chosen honesty, even when it would have been easier not to tell the truth. And I have chosen love, when I am met with even difficult truths as a parent. I asked for the truth, so part of trust-building is being able to meet it with love and care and respect when it is given.

I have learned there is no single ingredient that builds trust, but rather a collection of trust-building behaviours that teach us that trust can be both earned and given. Over the years, I've grown to appreciate that my dad and I were really saying the same thing about trust. Perhaps the hardest thing to trust people with is our hearts, as adoptees and as human beings. It's a worthy pursuit! So is trusting ourselves. It is the root system of love and bravery. All trust takes courage.

Pause & Reflect: Awareness to Action

As I reflect on the RELATIONSHIPS section of this guide...

What do I notice?

How do I feel?

What insights am I having?

What action would I like to take based on the awareness I'm gaining?

What are my next steps, if any?

RECLAIM
Belonging, integration, and empowerment

In the RECLAIM section of this guide, you are invited to explore:

- Reunion
- Belonging
- Forgiveness
- Heal Self-Abandonment
- Self-Compassion
- Genuine Gratitude
- Empowerment

REUNION

"Reunion has taught me that there is no way to remake your history or your family in the image you want. But there can be more, if you are willing to look for those stories that were lost—you might just find someone new to forgive, to love, to grow with."

—ZARA PHILLIPS

While an adoption reunion is a single moment in time, there may be many such reunion moments in an adoptee's experience of meeting various biological family members throughout the years. Still, it is also a single moment in time when that first meeting of a biological family member occurs.

There is an emotional journey before, during, and after any adoption reunion experience. There is also the decision, as an adoptee, to search for your biological roots in the first place. There are adoptees who never have to decide about searches or reunions, for example, in instances of open adoption or kin adoption where the original family is already known and not a mystery.

Reunions can be joyful, life-changing, and potentially very difficult. It is a vulnerable act to try and find, or be found by, original family members. You might learn about positive missing pieces of your history and identity, and you might learn very painful parts. You might learn origin stories and conception stories that are difficult to discover, or you might expand your understanding about missing pieces in your own story.

You may finally find a biological parent, only to learn they have no interest in meeting you. That was my experience when I originally learned the identity of my biological mother. I was told by the social worker that my mother did not want to meet me. It felt like a second abandonment and rejection, only this time I wasn't her newborn baby—I was a grown woman that she did not want to meet.

When that changed, and we did eventually meet over a year later, I learned more about why that was. But I had to sit in that painful feeling of being rejected, after the vulnerable attempt to search for her and after the excitement of discovering she was found. That she wasn't excited about being found, about the possibility of us being reunited, really hurt at the time.

Reunions are emotionally nuanced. I think of it as Pandora's box when deciding to search for biological roots. We don't know what we will find, how it will go, or where it will lead. It is a leap of faith to open the lid on all these unknowns.

Whether you have experienced a reunion in your own unique adoptee journey, or you are in the process of one, or have decided you don't ever wish for one, or perhaps it remains a possibility, may you remember love. Love for yourself, and love for all those involved. Anything is possible, even hard stuff, when love leads the way!

JOURNALING PROMPTS

Prompts if you have had a reunion experience...

What is my experience with reunion(s) with my biological family as an adoptee?

What do you remember about the first moments
of meeting?

How did this reunion affect my sense of identity?

Prompts if you have not had a reunion...

What feelings arise when I think about reaching out to my biological family?

What feelings arise when I think about not meeting my biological family (either by choice or circumstance)?

Would I like to have a reunion someday? Why
or why not?

_____

_____

_____

_____

_____

_____

_____

_____

_____

_____

What makes me feel whole and complete, with or
without a reunion experience as an adoptee?

_____

_____

_____

_____

_____

_____

_____

FROM THE PAGES OF MY JOURNAL

Eventually, the day I met my birth mother for the first time was one of the greatest, and emotionally complex, days of my life. The only other days in my life that opened my heart and whole being in such wide-open ways were the days my sons were born and I held them in my arms for the first time, and the day I held my dad in my arms when he died.

I met my birth mother, Diane, when I was thirty-one. We met at my dear friend Carrie's home, where her five-week-old baby girl and my mom were present. We had spent the morning figuring out what to wear. I never changed so many times before a single event in all my life. What do you wear when you are meeting your birth mother for the first time? My mom changed a few times too, as we supported each other to get dressed for this big moment in both of our lives. We were nervous and excited too.

I knew this moment would never be happening without the support of my mom. She had supported me all along with choosing to get my non-identifying adoption information, to applying for the search for my biological parents through the Children's Aid Society, to learning the identity of Diane, to the moment of waiting for the doorbell to ring to meet her for the first time. This whole process took over a decade.

Now, in a single moment, the doorbell rang, and I went to the front door to answer it. Carrie, my mom, and baby Sydney were in the living room giving me space to have this first moment on my own. I opened the door and stepped out on the front porch, where Diane and I immediately hugged each other. We were smiling and crying and taking each other in all at once. I will always remember the feeling of her first gaze, and her reaching up to trace my ears, and take my hands in hers, looking at each finger the way I did when holding my baby boys for the first time. Only she is doing this now, with her adult daughter, a stranger and not a stranger, all at once. As she stroked my hair and we hugged again, she whispered in my ear, "I love you," and I said, "I love you too." We've been learning, and choosing, what that means ever since.

BELONGING

"To this world you belong. To this moment, in this place where you already stand, something greater has ushered you."

—TOKO-PA TURNER

Belonging is a deep sense that you are accepted, valued, and connected for who you truly are without having to earn your place. It is more than just fitting in, which often means adjusting ourselves to meet others' expectations. When you have a sense of belonging, you feel like you matter and that you have a rightful place in the group, family, or relationship. There can be a fear of judgement from others that can compromise feelings of belonging and acceptance. It can take courage to acknowledge our desires and need to belong.

Belonging is often considered a core human need that contributes to our overall well-being, our resilience, and our ability to grow and thrive. As adoptees, there might be challenges with fitting in or feeling like we belong. If that happens, it is helpful to remember you can create feelings of belonging within yourself. Brené Brown says, "Belonging begins with self-acceptance; when we belong to ourselves, we can belong anywhere."

Simple affirmations can be reassuring and help cultivate your feelings of belonging, saying things to yourself like, *I carry a sense of belonging within me. I belong to the world.*

JOURNALING PROMPTS

When in my life do I feel a sense of belonging?
What makes this possible?

_____

_____

_____

_____

Where in my life, if any place, do I feel pressure to fit in
rather than be my authentic self?

_____

_____

_____

_____

How can I nurture feelings of belonging within myself?

_____

_____

_____

How do I belong to the world?

_____

_____

_____

_____

FORGIVENESS

"I'm sorry. Please forgive me. Thank you. I love you."

—HO'OPONOPONO MANTRA

Years ago, I read this beautiful Ho'oponopono mantra or prayer. Each phrase holds a specific healing intention, and it feels like a perfect mantra to have in our healing and forgiveness toolkit as adoptees.

"I'm sorry" acknowledges that something has happened that caused pain or disharmony.

"Please forgive me" asks for release and healing, even if you don't know the exact source of the pain.

"Thank you" expresses gratitude for the opportunity to make things right.

"I love you" restores connection, compassion, and wholeness.

I love this mantra and hope you do too!

Forgiveness can be freeing, and it is an essential element in the healing process. Forgiveness can be a profound and layered process for adoptees, as it might involve birth parents, adoptive parents, systems, even oneself. We might have to forgive our birth mothers for relinquishing us, our adoptive parents for not being perfect parents, ourselves for how we handled different aspects of our adoptee experience, and so forth. Forgiveness is part of all loving relationships, including the relationship we have with our self.

What is forgiveness? It is ultimately the process of releasing resentments from the past so that this resentment or hurt does not steal the joy away from the lives we are living now in the present. Forgiveness is not about condoning behaviours that may have hurt us or resulted in trauma wounds; it is about saying, I am releasing the deep resentment I may have about whatever happened. It means releasing the emotional hold any hurt may have over us and choosing peace versus bitterness. This is not easy to do, but it's worth the effort!

Dr. Gabor Maté says that, if the wound is healed, than there is nothing left to forgive. We have released ourselves from it, in part through the act of forgiveness.

JOURNALING PROMPTS

What would it feel like to forgive myself for things that were never mine to carry?

What might I gain from forgiving someone involved in my adoption journey?

Where in my life am I ready to practice releasing what no longer serves me, including resentments, hurtful experiences, or mistakes done to me or by me?

_____

_____

_____

_____

_____

_____

_____

_____

_____

_____

Forgiveness is not a destination, it's a practice. Where in my life am I ready to forgive more?

_____

_____

_____

_____

_____

HEAL SELF-ABANDONMENT

*"Freedom is not the absence of commitments, but
the ability to choose —and commit myself to—what
is best for me."*

—PAULO COELHO

Self-abandonment is not just a symptom; rather, it can be
a survival mechanism, something that feels familiar, when
feelings of shame or overwhelm, or any other feelings, might
feel too much. We can be hard on ourselves sometimes.
Self-abandonment might be a form of self-punishment,
or martyrdom, or a habit of putting other peoples' needs
before our own. We might not have learned how to show up
for ourselves fully. It can be a lifelong lesson and devotion
to do this.

As adoptees, there was a whole adoption system in place that
separated us from where we came from; that system, even
if well-intentioned, also separated us from parts of our self.
Healing begins when you acknowledge that system. I think,
as adoptees, it's possible that the part of us that was wounded
through being relinquished, given up, or taken, can quietly
get nervous when we start acting on our own behalf. Still, it's
valuable to take this action! We can do this lovingly by not
abandoning ourselves and our own needs. This is a slow and
meaningful path of returning to our self, again and again.

JOURNALING PROMPTS

What does self-abandonment mean to me? Where have I seen it show up in my life and relationships?

Are there times when I have silenced my feelings or needs to avoid conflict, or to feel loved and accepted?

What was I trying to protect when I started leaving
parts of myself behind?

_____

_____

_____

_____

_____

_____

_____

_____

_____

What do I feel when I begin to reconnect with parts of
myself that I've abandoned?

_____

_____

_____

_____

_____

_____

_____

How can I show up fully for myself at this time in my life?

FROM THE PAGES OF MY JOURNAL

Rightly or wrongly, sometimes the easiest person to abandon has often been myself. As a helper, wife, mother, daughter, friend, and adoptee, it's very familiar territory for me to love and serve the needs of others. This is also what was encouraged and socialized in me from an early age, to help others before myself. I was raised Catholic, where self-sacrifice was taught as a noble act, and one I often witnessed my mother role-model to me.

I recognize that being present for the needs of others can sometimes come at the expense of my own needs and self-care. I know I am not alone with this. I have worked in the burnout prevention space with helpers, healers, and caregivers for years, mostly with women, and I have heard a version of this same self-sacrificing story a thousand times.

I recognize this pattern of self-abandonment that can sometimes happen in my life and circumstances and choices. It is a winding road to truly come home to myself and commit to never abandoning myself again. The truth is, by default, that not abandoning myself will at times require abandoning the needs of someone else.

Being abandoned was an early wound; it is familiar deep within me. I don't want to abandon other people or what they need from me, especially the people I love the most. However, I have learned the hard way at times, the stakes are higher if I abandon myself.

I don't think there will be any prizes at the end of my life for abandoning myself for the sake of others, but I trust there is goodness that comes from showing up for myself and my own needs. I trust this goodness ripples out to the people I love, and in the world in some meaningful ways.

SELF-COMPASSION

"To honor and accept your adoptee story is to reclaim every piece of yourself with love and compassion."

—LYNDA MONK

I appreciate the work of Dr. Kristen Neff, who is a lead researcher in self-compassion. She says that self-compassion is treating yourself with the same kindness, care, and understanding you would offer a good friend when they're struggling. It involves choosing gentleness and understanding over harsh self-criticism when facing a pain or a failure or a mistake, things we all face in our lives from time to time!

Self-compassion reminds us that we are not alone with struggles or feelings we may be having, and I think this is so important as adoptees. The adoption experience can feel isolating at times, like others don't or can't truly understand what it's like to be adopted, unless they are adopted themselves. Self-compassion is a way of honoring our common humanity versus overly identifying with isolation. We can nourish self-kindness by being compassionate with ourselves and acknowledging that being imperfect is part of being human.

JOURNALING PROMPTS

What is a challenge I have faced as an adoptee? If my best friend had gone through it, what would I say to them?

What are three kind and supportive statements I would like to hear right now?

What are some ways I can be more compassionate and gentler with myself when I feel emotional pain, or get triggered by my adoption wound or any other emotional wound? Can I list three ways?

GENUINE GRATITUDE

"Adoption is the only trauma where the victims are
expected by the whole of society to be grateful."

—REVEREND KEITH C. GRIFFITH

For adoptees, there is both an overt and subtle pressure and expectation to be grateful. Grateful we were adopted, grateful we weren't left as orphans, grateful we weren't aborted, grateful we were chosen, grateful to be loved, grateful to have parents who "saved us," and the list of things to be grateful for can go on and on.

I believe gratitude can be tricky for adoptees. Not gratitude itself, but the pressure and expectation to be grateful for everything all the time. This can suppress or override all other feelings one might have or want to have besides, or beyond, being grateful.

There may be parts of your adoptee experience you aren't grateful for! You might have things that have hurt you or that you resent. For example, there are adoptees who do not feel grateful for their adoptive parents. Maybe they didn't feel loved and nurtured by their adoptive parents, or maybe they were abandoned again, or abused in their adoptive families, or treated like they'd been rescued and owed their adoptive parents something. There is no one-size-fits-all for what adoption looks like or how it goes when it has taken place.

Just like coming into any family, including a family of origin in non-adoptee situations, there can be healthy attachments, bonding, love and safety, and there can be broken attachments, abuse, and harm that can happen. This is true in any family, an adoptive one or otherwise. There can be things that are part of an adoptee's experience that make gratitude difficult; however, it is often expected anyway.

It's important to give yourself permission to feel gratitude in ways that are genuine for you! Don't hold your gratitude back. Look for shooting stars, random acts of kindness, and anything at all to be grateful for every single day.

JOURNALING PROMPTS

What is one thing about my adoptee experience that I feel truly grateful for?

_____

_____

_____

_____

_____

_____

_____

_____

_____

What is something that I have felt expected to feel grateful for that I might not actually feel grateful for?

_____

_____

_____

_____

_____

What is something about myself that I feel grateful for?

What role does gratitude play in my life?

_____

_____

_____

_____

_____

FROM THE PAGES OF MY JOURNAL

I have always been deeply grateful to have the love of my family and to even have my family, it could have been otherwise. I live a grateful life. Gratitude is my form of prayer. I believe in the healing power of gratitude. I have taught my sons the importance of gratitude. We have had many gratitude circles and sharing around our family dinner table. I have daily gratitude practices where I start and end my day bringing to my mind and heart all of the things I am grateful for in my life.

But amidst all this gratitude, it sometimes has suppressed other emotions I also feel, things like grief and sadness. I have learned to give myself permission to feel gratitude AND to feel many other emotions too. I have learned I can have deep love and gratitude for my family and still grieve the losses that have been part of my experience as an adoptee.

Gratitude is not some magical potion. Sometimes the magic happens when the wholeness and deeper truth of how I feel gets stirred in—gratitude mixed with sadness, mixed with joy, mixed with anger, or confusion, or wondering about what-if's, mixed with more gratitude.

AND, gratitude is magical, it makes everything better, it's like fairy dust sprinkled into life. It helps things sparkle just a little bit brighter.

EMPOWERMENT

*"The most common way people give up their power
is by thinking they don't have any."*

—ALICE WALKER

Being empowered is about having a sense of control or agency in our lives. By its very nature, no one else can give us this. It is something we must both discover and claim inside of ourselves and inside of our own lives.

Adoptees are not powerless. Adoptees are not pieces of a puzzle, taken from one family and moved over to another. We're not just waiting for all the pieces of our lives, and who we are, to fit together. Adoptees can feel empowered from within by deciding that identity is ours to define, and we can decide what parts of our stories shape us. We can carry multiple truths and histories all at once.

We can claim our personal agency, and impact our own lives and well-being in significant and fully empowered ways, at any time we choose to!

JOURNALING PROMPTS

What does being empowered mean to me?

What is one belief I hold today that helps me feel empowered?

How would I like to claim greater agency in my own life and circumstances?

_____

_____

_____

_____

_____

FROM THE PAGES OF MY JOURNAL

The greatest gift I've ever given myself was the moment (were the moments, as it has happened more than once) I decided to define my own life and take responsibility for it, not as an adoptee, or a this or that identity or role, but as an individual who is greater than the things that have happened in my life, good and bad, and instead I decided to be someone who can make things happen in my life. In that moment, I felt empowered. In that moment, I took agency of my life. This means I must believe in my ability to change, adapt, and grow in my own imperfect ways in a variety of situations. I must be willing to do what it takes to live an empowered life.

Pause & Reflect: Awareness to Action

As I reflect on the RECLAIM section of this guide...

What do I notice?

How do I feel?

What insights am I having?

What action would I like to take based on the awareness I'm gaining?

What are my next steps, if any?

REMEMBER
Honoring growth and wholeness

In the REMEMBER section of this guide, you are invited to explore:

- Birthday
- Child Within
- Goodness
- Loveable
- You Are Enough
- Self-Care
- Wholeness

BIRTHDAY

*"Birthdays as an adoptee are a sacred reminder
of your strength and journey. Each year, take time
to celebrate not just your birth but your resilience,
your courage to belong, and your power to define
your own life story."*

—LYNDA MONK

Birthdays can bring up a lot of emotions for adoptees. There
can be a heightened awareness that our birthday is also
potentially the anniversary of loss, even if never voiced. Even
if we weren't relinquished for adoption on the day we were
born, our birth itself, marked the beginning of eventually
being given away to another family. Adoptees can experience
birthdays differently at different stages of our lives as we
grow and continue to integrate the reality of being an adoptee
throughout our lives.

There are different thoughts and feelings I've had around
birthdays as an adoptee at various times in my life. For
instance, how I felt as a teenager on my birthday was
different than how I feel now. It has also changed being a
mother myself, always wanting birthdays to be a time of
celebration for and with our sons. I've also thought about how
my own birthday was not something my parents were part
of, which always felt strange in a way. Like all things with
adoption, birthdays are just another of the many moments
that can benefit from consideration and care.

JOURNALING PROMPTS

Have I experienced any extra emotion on birthdays as an adoptee? What have these feelings been?

_____

_____

_____

_____

_____

_____

_____

_____

What impact does being an adoptee have on how I have felt on my birthday over the years?

_____

_____

_____

_____

_____

_____

_____

What do I notice about my relationship to and with birthday celebrations, my own and for others?

What brings me joy on my birthday?

_____

_____

_____

_____

_____

_____

_____

_____

_____

FROM THE PAGES OF MY JOURNAL

I love birthday celebrations, especially the cake and presents, but...

There is no other day of the year, other than my birthday, that brings me into the heart of my emotions as an adoptee. There has never been one single birthday that I have not thought of my birth mother since that time when I was six years old and I learned I was adopted. My parents explained enough for me to know that it meant that I was not born to my mother, but that I was born to a different, unknown, mother. It was that other unknown mother who I thought of every birthday from that day forward. I also wondered if she thought of me.

I still think of her on my birthday, only now I have the joy of getting happy birthday messages from her, and two days later, I can send a birthday greeting her way.

CHILD WITHIN

"The child within is the keeper of our true self."

—LOUISE L. HAY

We all have a child within. It is that inner part of yourself that holds your earliest experiences, feelings, and memories from childhood. Your child within is like an emotional imprint of who you were as a child, carrying innocence, creativity, fears, hurts, met and unmet needs.

The inner child influences how we relate to ourselves and others, shaping emotional responses or reactions, self-worth and patterns in relationships. For adoptees who have experienced early loss or trauma, embracing the child within and listening to your inner child can be a powerful step toward healing and reclaiming wholeness. We're saying to ourselves, to our child within, "I see you, I remember you, I cherish you. You matter!"

My late journaling friend and colleague, Lucia Capacchione, was an expressive arts therapist and author of twenty books, including those focused on healing through inner child work. She wrote: "Your inner child is waiting patiently for you to show up and hold space for their story."

You can hold that space with your journaling as you write and listen within, witnessing and exploring your current story and your inner child story too. The following journaling prompts are inspired by Lucia's approach to her life's work.

JOURNALING PROMPTS

What does my inner child most want to tell me today, if I really listened?

_____

_____

_____

_____

_____

_____

_____

_____

_____

When did my inner child feel unseen or unheard? How can I offer comfort now?

_____

_____

_____

_____

_____

_____

_____

What are some ways I can create a safe, nurturing space for my younger self within me?

_____

_____

_____

_____

_____

How has my inner child shaped my beliefs about love, safety, and worth?

_____

_____

_____

_____

_____

What do I need to hear from my inner child to move toward healing?

_____

_____

_____

_____

_____

What does your inner child to need to hear from you now? Write them a letter.

_____

_____

_____

_____

_____

_____

FROM THE PAGES OF MY JOURNAL

Dear Child Within, you are precious. I can still remember your laughter, the ways you rode your bike down Shaver Street with your hands in the air, and how you wrote to pen pals all around the world, making connections with strangers through words and stories. I remember how your dad would take you for pizza (even when dinner was already in the oven), and your mom would make you wear snow pants and often ask "Are you warm enough?" Even though she wasn't big on hugs and snuggles and touch, all the things you longed for, she did know how to show you love each day.

I remember your pink painted room with Cinderella wallpaper. I remember all the fairy tales you believed in. I remember all the ways you wanted everyone's wishes to come true, even the impossible ones.

You, sweet girl, knew how to light up a room. Everyone was always so happy to see you. Always remember your radiance!

GOODNESS

"You are allowed to be both a masterpiece and a work in progress, simultaneously."

—SOPHIA BUSH

For adoptees, goodness can be a grounding truth. There can also be complex narratives about goodness and deservingness for adoptees, depending on your own unique circumstances. Being "good enough" can be freeing for adoptees! It can be a reminder that your value is not conditional on how well you're meeting anyone else's expectations or meeting their need for your goodness, to validate something in them, including your adoptive parents.

Sometimes, being good might not be how an adoptee tries to fit in or gain love or keep love. Adoptees might rebel, struggle, and go in directions other than "being good." They might isolate themselves, or push people away, or not fit in, or get lost in addictions. As a teenage girl, when I was trying so hard to be good, my younger brother was in his bedroom with a bottle of vodka under his bed, maybe in his own way, questioning if he was good enough.

Goodness itself is a bit nebulous, and it can be a high ground to get to at times. We don't have to have a higher standard of "goodness" as adoptees. We are simply individual works of art, masterpieces in progress, like everyone else.

JOURNALING PROMPTS

What does "being good enough" mean to me in my own words?

What rules or expectations about being "good" did I
learn growing up, and which ones no longer serve me?

When have I felt most at peace with or confident in
myself, without needing to change or improve?

_____

_____

_____

_____

_____

_____

_____

_____

_____

_____

_____

What would change in my life if I fully believed that I'm
already "good enough" just the way I am?

_____

_____

_____

_____

_____

_____

FROM THE PAGES OF MY JOURNAL

When I was a little girl, I always tried to be good. I was a good daughter, a good granddaughter, a good niece, a good friend, a good sister, a good student. Consciously, and probably subconsciously too, I wanted to be oh so good. I never wanted to give my parents any trouble. I wanted them to be proud of me (and they were); perhaps this is a desire all children have, for their parents to be proud of them.

I mostly never ever wanted them to regret that I was the daughter they got, the daughter they chose. I wondered how they chose me. Was there a row of babies to pick from, and I was the "good" one, so they reached for me and took me home to be their daughter? How did it all work, I wondered? I also wondered if every little girl was trying to be so good for the fear of losing love and belonging. For the fear of maybe being given up again.

Being good can be so tiring. Somewhere along the way I decided that I would be just good enough, and that would have to do. At this mid-season of my life, I am even curious about what it would be like to be less good, to even be a bit bad. I see women my age, and much younger women, talking about being "badass." Something sounds appealing to me about the idea of "being badass," even though I'm not sure I even know exactly what that means, but I would be curious to find out. Then again, maybe I already am "badass!"

LOVEABLE

*"Love isn't something you earn. It's
something you are."*

—KRISTIN NEFF

You are loveable. Believing one is loveable is something
adoptees might struggle with, given that they were given
away, or taken away, from their original families. This
relinquishment, or severing, can leave an adoptee possibly
wondering if they were loveable. They might even worry or
believe that they were unloveable (unwanted, rejected, flawed
in some way, etc.) and hence given up for adoption.

Adoption may shape us, but it does not diminish our
loveability. Our loveability is our inherent capacity to be
loved. It's not something to be earned or proved. We don't
have to audition for love, except maybe on dating apps, but I
digress. You are not just loveable; you are love itself.

JOURNALING PROMPTS

What would I say to my younger self to remind them
they are loveable no matter what?

What if being loveable isn't something to earn, but a truth to accept?

Who in my life has helped me feel truly loved? What did they say or do that made me feel loved and loveable?

_____

_____

_____

_____

_____

_____

_____

_____

_____

_____

What makes me feel loved and seen just as I am?

_____

_____

_____

_____

_____

_____

What do I absolutely love about myself?

YOU ARE ENOUGH

"You are enough for you. You are enough for the world. You are enough for anyone who deserves you."

—IYANLA VANZANT

A lot of people don't feel like they are enough, like they are fundamentally lacking or flawed in some way. This isn't just something an adoptee might feel. It is a normal and common human fear and emotion. That we aren't enough.

Other people might feel like they are too much. Too loud, or too talkative, or their dreams are too big, or that they are too much for other people to handle.

Neither of these things is true, we are both enough and not too much. This has nothing to do with us really, but rather what we think other people think of us, or what other people may have said to us about who we are. That does not mean that *is* who we are!

JOURNALING PROMPTS

How would I live if I knew I was already enough, before I did a single thing?

Describe what "enough" feels like using images, colours, or sensations.

What is something I love about myself that no one had to teach me?

_____

_____

_____

_____

_____

_____

Close your eyes, put your hand over your heart, and simply say, "I am enough."

Write a love letter to the part of you that believes this is true. If you can't access that part of you, write a love letter from a future version of you, who does believe this is true.

_____

_____

_____

_____

_____

_____

_____

_____

_____

FROM THE PAGES OF MY JOURNAL

At times I felt like I was too much for my family; too fast, too talkative, too active, too curious, too ambitious, too smart. My mom would often say, "You are too smart for your own good." Sometimes I felt too caring, too empathetic, too sensitive, too responsible, and too worried about other people.

As I got older, I started to reframe this feeling and say to myself, I'm not too much for this family, in fact, I was born so I could belong here. I was born so the fullness of me could expand this family into something more. Likewise, they turned me into someone more than I would have ever been without them.

One time, as an adult, when I was visiting my parents and slept in my childhood bedroom, I sat on the edge of the bed and quietly took in the room and some of the memories I had in it. I thought to myself, this room was made for me. I'm not, and never was, too much for it. I was always meant to be here, exactly as I am in our family. That was true then and it is true now.

SELF-CARE

*"True self-care is not salt baths and chocolate cake.
It's making a choice to create a life you don't need
to escape from."*

—BRIANNA WEIST

Adoption focuses on who cared for us in our childhoods and who couldn't care for us, for whatever reasons. Self-care is not about others caring for you, but rather how you care for yourself. Self-care is a skill set, a decision, and a devotional practice if we choose it to be. Self-care includes all the ways you tend to your emotional, physical, psychological, and spiritual well-being, how you care for your whole self. There is no one way to care for yourself, but rather many things you can do to be strong and nurtured in mind, body, heart, and spirit. Self-care is one of the ways you can show up for yourself and make yourself a priority. It reminds you that you can meet your own needs and that you don't have to be perfect to be cared for. It's a way you get to choose you! It's not necessarily a way to take a break from life, but rather a way to honor and tend to your own life. Self-care is a practice of remembering you, it is an act of love.

As Tama Kieves wrote, "When I eat blueberries, take a hot bath, journal, sleep, or read a novel, I am awakening the love within me. Where there is love, fear can't survive. Where there is love, there is the remembrance of bright abilities. The more I love myself, the more love I stream into my life."

JOURNALING PROMPTS

What are some of your favourite self-care practices?

_____

_____

_____

_____

_____

Who are you when you're not meeting the needs of others and you put your own self-care needs first?

_____

_____

_____

_____

_____

_____

_____

_____

_____

_____

_____

What fills your cup? How do you replenish and renew?

_____

_____

_____

_____

_____

_____

_____

How do you create a life that you love, a life that you
don't want to escape from?

_____

_____

_____

_____

_____

FROM THE PAGES OF MY JOURNAL

*Self-care has always been a topic I've been passionate
about and love learning about. I have taught about
it within burnout prevention workshops for helping
professionals, including fellow social workers, for years. It
is said that we teach what we most need to learn! In years
past, I would say self-care has been one of the biggest
lessons I have needed to learn. In more recent years, I
would say it has been my biggest teacher.*

WHOLENESS

"Healing does not mean the damage never existed. It means the damage no longer controls our lives, because we've reclaimed our wholeness."

—AKSHAY DUBEY

Wholeness comes from integrating all parts of where you come from and who you are, the glorious parts and the painful parts too. It includes the parts you have hidden or rejected, the parts you know and don't know yet, the parts you've been told were "too much" or "not enough." These parts get recognized and welcomed back into your awareness of your whole self. You can hold the wholeness of who you are with compassion and without judgment. We don't arrive at wholeness, but rather we deepen into it over time. Earlier in this journal, I wrote "to heal means to make whole." Our wholeness is evidence of our healing. As Tara Brach, author of Radical Acceptance, writes, "Healing begins the moment you stop trying to fix yourself and start remembering your wholeness."

JOURNALING PROMPTS

What parts of myself have I kept hidden, quiet, or ignored? How might I welcome them back?

What daily practices help me remember that nothing essential is missing from me?

_____

_____

_____

_____

_____

_____

_____

If I could draw my wholeness as a symbol, what would it look like?

_____

_____

_____

_____

_____

_____

How would I describe a moment in my life when I felt most whole?

_____

FROM THE PAGES OF MY JOURNAL

Years ago, I was floating naked in the ocean off a secluded beach on the big island of Hawaii. I was alone and had left Peter and the boys playing in the shallow water together, splashing and looking for sea turtles. My parents had just been with us for two weeks, and it was the biggest trip they had ever taken in their lives.

During this time together, it became very evident that my dad was declining with Alzheimer's disease. I could see parts of him were disappearing and they were not going to return. As I was floating in the water, I could feel the emotional weight of grief in the water with me as my tears mixed with the salt water of the sea.

I felt a piece of my dad's wholeness was leaving and a new part of my own was going to have to be found. I knew I was going to have to help my parents sell their home of forty-plus years, downsize, move, get care, and so on. I knew there was big and heartful work ahead. It felt scary.

While I floated alone, held by the ocean beneath me, I felt the sea whisper in my ear, "I've got you. I will hold you above water, as you witness your dad submerge into Alzheimer's." I realized love has to be willing to hold the wholeness of each other, even the missing parts. I realized, I have to love the wholeness of myself too, even the parts I haven't met yet.

Pause & Reflect: Awareness to Action

As I reflect on the REMEMBER section of this guide...

What do I notice?

How do I feel?

What insights am I having?

What action would I like to take based on the awareness I'm gaining?

What are my next steps, if any?

RADIANCE
Living with love and making peace

In the RADIANCE section of this guide, you are invited to explore:

- Remember Your Radiance
- Practice Acceptance
- Open to Self-Love
- Learn to Savor
- Seek Happiness
- Make Peace
- Be a Love Story

REMEMBER YOUR RADIANCE

*"You are not here to fix yourself. You are here to
remember yourself—your radiance, your origin,
your Infinity."*

—HARIJIWAN

You are radiant. You shine who you are out into our world.
You are not separate from your origin story, nor does it define
all of who you are. You're infinite. You're here for a reason
and for time beyond time. How you arrived here is only the
beginning; how you live, how you love, how you stay open
to the whole of life and the whole of yourself, is the greatest
part of our life journeys.

Your radiance is like a giant sunbeam. You don't ever have
to dim your light. You are a sovereign shining star. I believe
there is a holy remembrance of our radiance that is needed
as adoptees, as human beings, living at this time in human
history. We belong to generations that came long before us,
we are part of a lineage of light that will live long beyond
us. This is not just about biology, or where we arrive, or our
experiences; it is bigger than all of that. There is an entire
galaxy of time and space and luminosity that we belong to,
we were born to shine!

JOURNALING PROMPTS

What does it mean to me to remember my radiance?

What makes me feel most alive, bright, and fully myself?

What parts of myself have I dimmed to feel accepted or safe, and what would it feel like to let them shine again?

What do others often see in me that I sometimes forget about myself?

What message of hope or encouragement would I offer
to another adoptee still searching for their light?

_____

_____

_____

_____

_____

When I think of the power of my inner light, I notice...
or I feel...

_____

_____

_____

_____

_____

_____

FROM THE PAGES OF MY JOURNAL

Somewhere along the way in life, I decided I am here to shine. I try my very best to do what it takes to let my radiance be fully alive in me and this life I am living. On the days when I forget this or don't feel very radiant, I play Rihanna's inspiring song "Diamonds." I put my AirPods in and I walk, and walk, and take in her lyrics and I remember my own shining, my own call to radiance. As she sings over and over again, "shine bright like a diamond, we're beautiful like diamonds in the sky," I start singing too. I get myself picked up and remember my radiance.

Sometimes, when I walk along the beaches where we live (on an island), I will pick up a stone along the shoreline. I will hold it in my hands, dip it in the ocean water, rub it smooth, and see it go from a dirt-covered stone to a shining, radiant rock. Its radiance was there all along. It just needed some of the dirt that was covering it to be removed or smoothed off. I think we are a lot like that as people—our experiences, mistakes, wounds, losses, can layer dirt on us and we can forget our radiance under all of that, but we can also dust away the dirt, and remember and reveal our innate shining selves.

Radiance is energy, and it is never just for us, it is a like a magic beam of light that goes from one person to another. We need each other to shine, since we all get our radiance from each other in some small way.

I am here to "shine bright like a diamond." And so are you!

PRACTICE ACCEPTANCE

"Adoption begins with loss. Healing begins with acceptance."

—NANCY VERRIER

There are many things we must accept along the way in our lives. Some situations or realities are easier to accept than others. This is not unique to being an adoptee. However, adoptees often walk a unique emotional and psychological path that asks us to grow into acceptance, not as resignation, but as a deep and evolving integration of truth, loss, identity, and love. Acceptance doesn't have to mean that everything is okay or perfect, rather it means recognizing any impact being adopted has had on us with compassion and self-love.

JOURNALING PROMPTS

What have I had to grow to accept (even if not fully accept, but at least partially accept) as an adoptee?

How does acceptance support my healing and growth as an adoptee? How does it make me feel?

What have I decided not to accept because it's what is best for me to do?

_____

_____

_____

_____

What does self-acceptance mean for me as an adoptee?

_____

_____

_____

_____

_____

FROM THE PAGES OF MY JOURNAL

I never knew I was on a journey towards acceptance as an adoptee. I just thought I accepted the fact that I was adopted. But the more steps I took forward in my life as an adoptee, the more peace I realized there was to make with the subtle quiet sadness that lived inside me all my happy life. So quiet, I didn't even know it was there.

OPEN TO SELF-LOVE

"There is you and you. this is a relationship. this is the most important relationship."

—NAYYIRAH WAHEED

It's a great feeling to be loved. It's a great feeling to count on love, to trust it and rely on it, and relish in it. It is often something we might seek outside of ourselves, especially if a person is testing to see if they are indeed loveable, as an adoptee might do, as any human being might do. Receiving love from others is beautiful, and opening to receiving love from ourselves is exquisite. It is a love that can last a lifetime, if we tend to it. There is a very powerful presence of, and capacity for, self-love that lives within us. You might have to dig for it or sing it from a mountaintop or look yourself in the eye while seeing your reflection in the mirror, put your hands over your heart and declare confidently: "I love you." In that moment, of receiving your own love, you might weep, for the power of self-love can open dormant places in your heart and whole being. Say it again like you mean it: "I love you, I've got you."

JOURNALING PROMPTS

Buddha said: "You yourself, as much as anybody in the entire universe, deserve your love and affection." How do I show myself love and affection?

How can I be more loving with myself and less judgemental or harsh?

Is there some part of my adoptee story that needs a dose of self-love added to it?

What love is waiting to awaken within me?

_____

_____

_____

_____

_____

_____

FROM THE PAGES OF MY JOURNAL

_When I recently ran my first, and possibly my only, 10K
race, it was something I had not trained for. I had made
a commitment to myself to enter the race. It was a goal I
had that was more broadly about challenging myself to do
something to get more active and start taking better care
of my physical health. I had three goals for the race: get
to the starting line, get to the finish line, and don't die or
injure myself between those two places. As I was running,
I had a moment where I decided that I was not going to
let myself walk and I was going to push to run the whole
10K, despite never having done this before. As I kept on
running, and pushing up a bit of a hill, there was an instant
when I felt emotional, and felt tears run down my cheeks
as I kept going. It was a moment of realizing that this race
was an act of self-love, it was also me versus me. It wasn't
me versus the hundreds of other runners who were also
in the race. I felt a deep knowing that part of self-love
is in the moments I truly show up for myself and what is
important to me. When I was running that race, I could feel
self-love pulsing through me every time my feet hit the
road beneath me. This love felt so good, it moved me to
tears._

LEARN TO SAVOR

"Instructions for living a life: Pay attention. Be astonished. Tell about it."

—MARY OLIVER

I believe we are here to try our very best to savor these lives we have been given. There are surely stressful and unjust things that happen which make it difficult to savor life at times. There can be tough things to navigate, and circumstances beyond one's control that can make savoring seem like a very lofty goal, especially if you are in high stress and survival mode for whatever reason(s). But if and when we can, let's try to savor our lives!

To savor life as an adoptee means fully embracing and finding the richness in the experiences, relationships, and moments that make up your life, while also honoring the complexity that adoption can bring. It's about allowing joy, gratitude, and meaning to exist alongside the grief, loss, and identity questions that may also be part of your adoptee story.

JOURNALING PROMPTS

What are some moments from my life so far that I truly savor, cherish or treasure? Make a list of these moments.

In what ways has my journey as an adoptee given me a unique perspective on what matters most to me, on what I want to savor?

What are some small everyday pleasures or moments to savor that I sometimes rush past?

_____

_____

_____

_____

_____

_____

_____

_____

If I could design a "savoring ritual" to practice once a week, what would it look like? How can you engage your senses in this practice?

_____

_____

_____

_____

_____

_____

_____

FROM THE PAGES OF MY JOURNAL

I have studied a lot about mindfulness and try my best to live a mindful life. Mindfulness teaches that we don't live in the past and we don't live in the future and that our true power lives in being fully present in the now. The more I relish what's here now...the simple pleasures, moments of gratitude, snuggling our dog, watching a sunrise, feeling the rain on my skin, journaling with my morning coffee, it all reminds me I'm here now.

I feel most at peace when I find things to savor and appreciate in the simple moments in my everyday life. I also find things to savor about being an adoptee. I think my life is richer as an adoptee because I have truly tried to understand how this experience has shaped me and my life, including my relationships. I try to savor everything that has been true in my life as an adoptee, even the hard parts. I am savoring the privilege of being here now, writing this adoptee guide and journal to share with you. This moment would not be possible if I weren't an adoptee, I want to savor what is possible because I am.

SEEK HAPPINESS

"The purpose of our lives is to be happy."

—DALAI LAMA

I know happiness is not a given in life and that many people struggle to feel happy. Happiness is not frivolous, but it is purposeful. Why am I talking about happiness in this adoptee guide? There are multiple studies that show adoptees have higher rates of mental health diagnoses than non-adoptees, including clinical depression and suicidal behaviours. One study, done through the US Department of Health and Human Services, reports that 9% of adopted adolescents have been diagnosed with depression, compared to 4% of their non-adopted peers. Other studies have shown that adoptees are three to four times more likely to attempt suicide than non-adopted individuals. These findings suggest that there needs to be attention paid to the mental health of adoptees, through understanding some of the vulnerabilities and risk factors that adoptees might face.

Seeking happiness serves to mitigate these risks by knowing that, as an adoptee, you have the right to your happiness, and that you can do things to seek and create it in your life. It might take a little extra effort to do that, depending on your own unique circumstances, but if you make your happiness a priority and take a stand for it, you are more likely to create the circumstances and cultivate any support you might need to make it so.

To be adopted is to carry many truths, but always one remains: You are worthy of happiness! You deserve a happy life not because of where you came from, but because you are here.

JOURNALING PROMPTS

How does my adoption story shape the way I think
about happiness?

_____

_____

_____

_____

_____

_____

_____

_____

How do I define happiness for myself, not what others
expect, but what feels true to me?

_____

_____

_____

_____

_____

_____

_____

_____

In what ways does claiming happiness feel like reclaiming a part of myself?

What is one of my happiest moments related to my adoptee journey?

FROM THE PAGES OF MY JOURNAL

Without a doubt, one of my happiest moments related to my adoptee journey was the day I married my husband. We got married at our home, down at the beach, with about eighty family members and friends present. We married on September 11, 2004, which was also my thirty-fifth birthday. I was walked down the grassy slope from our house down to the beach, which served as our wedding aisle, with everyone looking up from down below.

What made this an extraordinary moment for me, in addition to marrying the man I love, was that both of my mothers walked me down the aisle! Peter, his dad, and my dad were waiting for us at the bottom of the "aisle". It was one of the happiest moments in my life so far. I had my mom on one side of me and my birth mom on the other, and I felt complete. I felt like I was in a dream, and could barely believe it was happening. It gave having a "fairy-tale wedding" a whole new meaning!

This was in the early years after finding and meeting my biological mom for the first time. It was during the time when her family still didn't know I existed. She explained the reason for her travel from Ontario to BC by saying that she was attending a "friend's wedding." However, what was true was that she was a guest of honor at my wedding, her daughter's wedding. I am the only child she's ever had, the only wedding where she could be the "mother of the bride," one of them at least.

I will be forever grateful to my parents for the loving way they expanded the heart and circle of our family to include Diane, on this very special day and for many other special moments we have shared together in the twenty-plus years since then. My parent's love and inclusion of Diane in our family has always felt like one of the greatest gifts of love they have given to me.

MAKE PEACE

"Make peace with your broken pieces."

—R. H. SIN

Peace doesn't mean all the pieces of your adoptee story and life experiences are all neatly in place. It means you've made a home within yourself, just as you are. Peace isn't about forgetting any part of your adoptee story, but rather, it's about finding peace with remembering and acknowledging the wholeness of your journey. Peace may be the hardest thing we ever make in our lives! The peace we find must come from within, and that is big work to do.

JOURNALING PROMPTS

What has brought me peace as an adoptee at different times in my life?

What brings me a sense of peace on stressful or emotionally challenging days?

What parts of my adoption story still feel unsettled, if any, and what might peace look like in those areas?

What is something I can let go of, not because it's wrong, but because it no longer serves my inner peace?

What does inner peace mean to me at this time
in my life?

FROM THE PAGES OF MY JOURNAL

*As adoptees, as individuals, we work to find and make
peace in the context of our lives, circumstances, and
the world we're in. Our world is not a peaceful place. It
is currently particularly tumultuous. Most people do not
feel that peaceful and there is a lot of anxiety floating all
around us.*

*I feel most at peace in nature, walking in the forest, being
at the beach, watching the full moon rise over Fulford
Harbour. I feel most at peace when I focus on noticing
beauty and practicing gratitude, and when I put my energy
and intention into things that I can control or influence in
some way. I prioritize my peace, and I know it is a privilege
to have it!*

*I've learned a lot about peace throughout my life by
observing other people and their lives. Years ago, early
in my social work career while I was working in child
welfare, I remember going to a client's home. This woman
was a single mother and had five children. Her home was
completely chaotic, filled with hoarding and disarray and
dirty diapers across the floor. There was an overflowing
cat litterbox just inside the front door and cigarette butts*

on the table that had missed the ashtray. It was an unsafe environment for children, including her toddler, who was crawling on the floor. Two of her older children had already been apprehended and put in foster care more than once. Not due to overflowing everything, but due to abuse from one of their mother's partners.

During one of our home visits, I offered to help her start cleaning up, and she looked at me like "Why would I do that, things are perfectly fine." She said something to me that I will never forget, something that I took with me when I visited many other clients in their homes after that. She said, "I feel most at peace when there's chaos all around me, it's the only thing I've ever known."

In that moment, I learned a valuable lesson that inner peace is a subjective state; so is the cleanliness of an outer environment! It didn't mean her home, and circumstances, didn't need some cleaning up for safety's sake for her and her young family. But I knew it had to be a gentle process, and it had to start with top-layer things that posed potential risk. For example, the boxes of overflowing clothes, and other things that were everywhere, I thought to myself, they may just need to stay there, they may just be her only form of peace.

I don't know what ever happened for that woman and her family in the years that followed our work together. She would be an older woman now, with her kids grown. She likely has grandchildren and maybe even great-grandchildren, and they might come to her home and step over her boxes and chaos, and they might live in homes with overflowing ashtrays, and dangerous circumstances, too. Their own chaos might be the only peace they've ever known. They might be working hard to make peace with their mother, and the difficult childhoods they had.

I've grown to believe that, throughout our lives, we all have things and people to make peace with at times, including ourselves.

BE A LOVE STORY

"Adoptees share the unique experience of carrying the rejection of relinquishment while also trying to balance the natural human need to be loved and known for who we are."

—LAURA SUMMERS

Our lives are defined both by what we have lost and what we carry. Our whole lives are a story. You can be the hero of your own life story. Heroes grieve and love. They have courage, perseverance, empathy, and determination. They also go through some sort of transformational journey gaining wisdom, strength, or a deeper understanding of themselves. The moral of the story in any hero's journey is not about winning, but about becoming. As adoptees, we can choose the presence of love as part of our hero's journey. We can give the love we seek and be transformed by it. We can choose to live our lives as a love story. You can be a love story!

JOURNALING PROMPTS

What have I learned about love and connection through my journey as an adoptee?

How does love show up in ways that I might not always notice through things like kindness, protection, listening, generosity, presence, etc.?

_____

_____

_____

_____

_____

_____

_____

_____

_____

_____

_____

What is my love language? How do I like to show love and how do I like to receive love?

_____

_____

_____

_____

_____

How can my life be a love story?

_____

_____

_____

_____

_____

FROM THE PAGES OF MY JOURNAL

A love note to you...

Dear Fellow Adoptee:

I want to send some love your way, just because, from one adoptee to another. I believe love flows to you, from you, and all around you. Like the subtle, beautiful, layered, soft and strong light-infused heart on the cover of this book, may you love and accept all your layers and experiences with grace and tender care. May you cherish this life you are living, including the fullness of your experiences as an adoptee. May you love yourself wholeheartedly each and every day, you deserve this love. You are enough and never too much. You are here, now. Thank you for reading and writing and reflecting. I believe it creates a ripple effect of healing out into our world, our families, and beyond. Journaling is a way to know, grow, and care for yourself that can spread a silent love wave from your head to heart to hand, filling you with hope and healing. Thank you and know you are loved just for being here!

Write from the heart,
Lynda

Pause & Reflect: Awareness to Action

As I reflect on the RADIANCE section of this guide...

What do I notice?

How do I feel?

What insights am I having?

What action would I like to take based on the awareness I'm gaining?

What are my next steps, if any?

Conclusion

*"Often when you think you're at the end
of something, you're at the beginning of
something else."*

—FRED ROGERS

Endings as Beginnings

I've never liked endings. I much prefer beginnings and all
the good stuff in between. But endings are essential parts of
any new beginnings. We have many beginnings in our lives,
small ones, monumental ones, and all the transitions and
emotional adjustment that goes with them. As adoptees, we
each have our unique set of endings and beginnings in our
adoption stories.

I hope this adoptee guide and journal has helped you connect
with your own story, or parts of it, in fresh, empowering, and
self-loving ways. I wish you much goodness on the part of
your story that is not yet written or lived.

*"When you own your story, you get to write
the ending."*

—BRENÉ BROWN

An adoption journey is not defined by one moment; rather it's
a living story of growth, reclamation, and becoming whole.
What I know about you if you are here, reading this, having
written and reflected by now, is that you are committed to
living your best life. You are living an intentional life where
healing, wholeness, and growth matter to you! You are brave
and willing to reflect on your life with as much honesty,
vulnerability, and openness as you can in this moment and
the next. Take a moment to celebrate YOU and acknowledge
all you have done in the pages of this journal, and/or in
your companion journal that you might have kept as you
have gone through the seven healing pathways offered

here, including: roots, recognition, resilience, relationships, reclaim, remember, and radiance.

You have done healing work with the help of this guide and journal. You have reclaimed parts of you that have been in the shadows, or that you have not looked at recently or ever. It's courageous to meet ourselves and our life experiences as adoptees in this way. You are courageous. You are brave!

Thank you for trusting me as your guide. Thank you for trusting yourself. You are always the expert on your own experience. Thank you for your willingness to explore, stretch, open, and expand. Willingness is everything.

Thank you for trusting yourself to live true, to live whole. You've got this! Life is here for you. I hope this guide has helped you connect with both your wholeness and your story. Your story matters. You matter.

ALL THAT WE ARE IS STORY

"All that we are is story. From the moment we are born to the time we continue on our spirit journey, we are involved in the creation of the story of our time here. It is what we arrive with. It is all we leave behind."

—RICHARD WAGAMESE

Own your story, and remember, adoption is the beginning, and only part of your story; it is not the whole story. You are an adoptee and so much more. YOU are a whole story.

All that we are is story. Our stories can have new chapters at any time. We can rewrite past stories. We can't change what happened to us, but we can change how we tell, see, and feel about what happened to us, we can bring new ways of seeing to the experience. We can choose how we think about our stories and how we tell them too. Our story may not be the same as others' stories of the same experience; that doesn't make it better or worse, it just makes it our own. We see the world through our own lens. We can live our stories in our own ways, on our own terms. As Richard Wagamese said, "It is what we arrive with. It is all we leave behind."

AFTERWORD

JULIANA J BRUNO

Author of *Reasons to Live: An Interactive Guide to Healing and Overcoming Suicidal Thoughts and How to Help Others Survive*
Host of the *I Care About You* Podcast
https://www.julianajbruno.com/

The Adoptee's Guide to Healing, Wholeness & Growth radiates with compassion, authenticity, and profound inner wisdom. Author Lynda Monk, MSW, RSW, CPCC, invites the reader to reexamine their story, not with judgment or "shoulds," but with curiosity, kindness, and real human vulnerability. This book is a rare and precious combination of whole-person healing modalities and practices.

Beyond inspiring reflection, the book offers concrete practices (journaling prompts, affirmations, compassionate reflections) that readers can actually use. It's not just theory; it's a workshop for the soul. The author's sensitivity to trauma, depression, grief, identity, and healing means the book speaks to a broad and diverse range of readers beyond those who are part of the adoptee experience. It holds space for those often overlooked by mainstream self-help, and that's a beautiful gift.

This book was a profound healing experience for me. I was adopted at birth, and my origin story, always known to me, brought with it a lot of inner pain and suffering. Although I grew up in a family with loving parents, my self-identity was woven tightly around ideas of worthlessness and shame, not from any doing of my adoptive parents but from the stigma and social beliefs around being "given up," " not real," and "an outsider." *The Adoptee's Guide to Healing, Wholeness & Growth* spoke to me directly and compassionately about my struggles and gave me a roadmap out of the self-deprecating jungle I had long been trapped in.

The Adoptee's Guide to Healing, Wholeness & Growth is a gentle, powerful companion for inner work, and a must-read for anyone yearning to move from self-judgment to self-compassion, from pain to growth, from fear to love. I wholeheartedly recommend it.

RESOURCES & SUGGESTED READING

The following are among the many books I've read about adoption, trauma, and the healing power of journal writing, and some are referenced in *The Adoptee's Guide to Healing, Wholeness & Growth*.

Early Books on Adoption

Lifton, BJ. (2009) *Lost and Found: The Adoption Experience.* Ann Arbor, MI: University of Michigan Press.

Sorosky, A., Baran, A., & Pannor, R. (1989). *The Adoption Triangle: Sealed or Opened Records: How They Affect Adoptees, Birth Parents, and Adoptive Parents.* San Antonio, TX: Corona Publishing Co.

Verrier, N. (2003). *The Primal Wound: Understanding the Adopted Child.* Baltimore, MD: Gateway Press.

Adoption Memoirs

Engel, L. (2022). *You'll Forget This Ever Happened: Secrets, Shame, and Adoption in the 1960s.* Berkeley, CA: She Writes Press.

McGue, J. (2021). *Twice a Daughter: A Search for Identity, Family, and Belonging.* Berkeley, CA: She Writes Press.

Writing to Heal & Grow

Adams, K. (1990). *Journal to the Self: Twenty-Two Paths to Personal Growth.* New York, NY: Warner Books.

Baldwin, C. (1991). *One to One: A New Updated Edition of the Classic Self-Understanding Through Journal Writing.* New York, NY: M. Evans and Company.

Capacchione, L. (1989). *Recovery of Your Inner Child: The Highly Acclaimed Method for Liberating Your Inner Self.* New York, NY: Simon & Schuster.

Chapman, J. (2015). Original copyright 1991. *Journaling for Joy: Writing Your Way to Personal Growth and Freedom – The Workbook.* Van Nuys, CA: New Castle Publishing Company, Inc.

DeSalvo, L. (1999). *Writing as a Way of Healing: How Telling Our Stories Transforms Our Lives.* Boston, MA: Beacon Press.

Maisel, E. & Monk, L. (Eds.). (2022). *The Great Book of Journaling: How Journal Writing Can Support a Life of Wellness, Creativity, Meaning, and Purpose.* Coral Gables, FL: Mango Publishing/Conari Press.

Marinella, S. (2017). *The Story You Need to Tell: Writing to Heal from Trauma, Illness, or Loss.* Novato, CA: New World Library.

Matousek, M. (2017). *Writing to Awaken: A Journey of Truth, Transformation, and Self-Discovery.* Oakland, CA: Reveal Press.

Pennebaker, J. W. & Evans, J. (2014). *Expressive Writing – Words that Heal.* Enumclaw, WA: Idyll Arbor.

Weldon, M. (2001). *Writing to Save Your Life: How to Honor Your Story Through Journaling.* Center City, MN: Hazelden.

Books on Trauma, Shame, Vulnerability, Resiliency, Self-Compassion, Acceptance & Belonging

Brach, T. (2004). *Radical Acceptance: Awakening the Love That Heals Fear and Shame.* New York: NY: Penguin Random House.

Brown, B. (2010). *The Gifts of Imperfection: Let Go of Who You Think You're Supposed to Be and Embrace Who You Are.* Center City, MN: Hazelden Publishing.

Kieves, T. (2025). *Learning to Trust Yourself: Breaking Through the Blocks That Hold You Back.* New York, NY: St. Martin's Publishing Group.

Levine, P. (1997). *Waking the Tiger: Healing Trauma.* Berkeley, CA: North Atlantic Books.

Maté, G. & Maté, D. (2022). *The Myth of Normal: Trauma, Illness, and Healing in a Toxic Culture.* Toronto, ON: Knopf Canada/ Penguin Random House.

Neff, K. (2015). *Self-Compassion: Stop Beating Yourself Up and Leave Insecurity Behind.* New York, NY: William Morrow/ HarperCollins.

Seligman, M. (2011). *Flourish: A Visionary New Understanding of Happiness and Well-Being.* New York, NY: Free Press/Simon & Schuster.

Turner, Toko-pa (2017). *Belonging: Remembering Ourselves Home.* Salt Spring Island, BC: Her Own Room Press.

van der Kolk, B. (2015). *The Body Keeps the Score: Brain, Mind, and Body in the Healing of Trauma.* New York, NY: Penguin Books.

"It is through our names that we first place ourselves in the world. Our names, being the gift of others, must be made our own."

—RALPH ELLISON

ABOUT THE AUTHOR

LYNDA MONK, MSW, RSW, CPCC
(name at birth: Laura Rosehart)

Lynda Monk is an adoptee and an avid journal writer. She was born in Kitchener and placed for adoption five days later in London, Ontario, Canada. This was in 1969, during the era when adoption records were closed and birth mothers were told to forget their babies were ever born. She is passionate about the healing power of writing and stories reclaimed.

Lynda is a Registered Social Worker, Certified Professional Co-Active Coach, and leader of the International Association of Journal Writing (IAJW.org), an inspirational and educational community for journal writers worldwide. She is known for her profound insights into the therapeutic and life-changing power of journaling. She is the co-editor and co-author of several books, including *The Great Book of Journaling*; *Transformation Journaling for Coaches, Therapists, and Clients*; *Writing Alone Together*, and others.

She lives with her family on Salt Spring Island, BC, Canada, where she is currently writing *Another Thousand Kisses: An Adoptee's Memoir* (working title).

CONNECT WITH ME

We've been on an important journey together through this guide!

I would be grateful to hear your experiences with this guide as a fellow adoptee, or as someone who supports adoptees.

I welcome all reader feedback—what was helpful, what was hard, what impacted you the most, what was your journaling journey like and anything else you might like to share.

Feel welcome to connect!

You can find me here:

Email me: lynda@iajw.org or lynda@lyndamonk.com

Join me on other social media channels, including the following:

www.instagram.com/iajw_org

www.linkedin.com/in/lyndamonk

www.youtube.com/lyndamonk

Join my Facebook group especially for journal writers

https://www.facebook.com/groups/journalwritingtribe

Visit my websites:

https://lyndamonk.com – my speaker and author website

https://IAJW.org – International Association for Journal Writing

Subscribe to my free Journaling Museletter and receive ongoing inspiration for your journaling journey and some free gifts too! You can sign-up here: https://iajw.org/museletter

A special request...

Please post a review of *The Adoptee's Guide for Healing, Wholeness & Growth* on Amazon or Goodreads. Every reader review goes a long way to helping make books like this more accessible to others. Thank you for helping make a difference!

A note to event organizers...

I love speaking at events especially for adoptees, their families and for adoption serving organizations. I also love being a guest on adoptee podcasts and other virtual events. Please consider me as a speaker or presenter for your event or group. You can find all my speaker details at www.lyndamonk.com Thank you.